CATCHING FIRE

Men's Renewal and Recovery Through Crisis

About the author:
  Merle Fossum is a husband, father, tree farmer, outdoorsman, and writer. He is co-founder of the Family Therapy Institute in St. Paul, Minnesota where he is a family therapist.

CATCHING FIRE

Men's Renewal and Recovery Through Crisis

Merle Fossum

HAZELDEN

First published August 1989.

ISBN: 0-89486-605-2
Library of Congress Catalog Card Number: 89-83559

Printed in the United States of America.

Editor's Note:

Hazelden Educational Materials offers a variety of information on chemical dependency and related areas. Our publications do not necessarily represent Hazelden or its programs, nor do they officially speak for any Twelve Step organization.

Dedication

In gratitude for the creative spirit in those first desperate men who reached out to each other and developed the Twelve Steps of Alcoholics Anonymous. They discovered a path of transformation and showed that recovery is possible. Their Steps now lead the way for millions who struggle with life problems.

Contents

Preface

In the hundreds of hours spent writing this book, an image kept returning to me like a companion. I saw the recovering men in my personal life, my profession, and those who generously volunteered their stories for this book. Nothing is more encouraging in my own journey than seeing another man on fire with a renewed spirit. He often feels lucky to be alive and may say, "I feel like a real person for the first time in my life." He took the risk to believe he could change. He has more self-esteem than ever before. He listens to his inner voice and has a spiritual life. He has a new reservoir of energy, has faced pain, and uses it to grow into a stronger, healthier man.

I return to this image because it is so encouraging. I know that once a man awakens he can begin profound change. But we are social creatures; we need others to help discover the best in ourselves. Just as I gained strength for my recovery by knowing others on this path, I hope this book will be a companion for you, offering encouragement and direction.

I also return to the image of those recovering men because I know how lonely we have been, how crucial relationships are for growth, how fully we expect to be alone, and how surprising it can be when we connect with others. My main goal in writing this book is to provide an antidote to that loneliness; to offer it as a companion on the journey for recovery. Perhaps sometimes it will also serve as a compass, helping you to find direction, and sometimes as a bridge, helping you move to the next part of the journey.

The companion may be found in the stories of other men's experiences; the compass in the ideas and concepts about recovery; and the bridge in the practical parts of this book, the concrete suggestions for how to do it. Most chapters contain a mixture of all three elements but Chapters One, Two, and Four are less concrete, so I included exercises at the end of these chapters to help actualize them. I hope you find hope in the stories of others told here, and I hope you find parts of your own story in theirs.

Several people helped me write this book. Norman Vinnes and Rene Schwartz were supportive, devoting their valuable time to reading the manuscript, making suggestions, and discussing their ideas with me. Jim D'Aurora and Denise D'Aurora took hours from their busy schedules to read and comment on the draft as it developed, and they gave their valuable moral support. Mavis Fossum's belief and encouragement continues to be immensely helpful to me. Craig Nakken's help on a major section helped me decide what I wanted to say. Alan Braverman's interest and willing initiative helped me move forward with important parts. The men who talked about their recovery for this book shall remain anonymous, but I want to say thanks to each one for the gift of his story, which made this book richer. I appreciate the interest and work of my daughters, Linnea and Thyra, who helped with proofreading. Brian Lynch, my editor, believed in this book and helped clarify its message. In addition to the individuals I've specifically named, I want to acknowledge the major contribution of my clients. None of their stories are specifically included, although what they taught me is reflected in this book. I am grateful for the moral support of my esteemed colleagues at the Family Therapy Institute; they accommodated my need to set aside some of my clinical duties so I could write.

CHAPTER 1

Eye Opening

Adversity introduces a man to himself.
—Anonymous

Mike sat in my office on the blue-striped couch and said, "I was on just one track my whole life. When I was in school, I competed for top grades and for captain of the baseball team. I always got what I worked for. After graduation, I competed to reach the top of the ladder at a major computer corporation. Only the best was good enough there. All other needs came second, including friendships and fun. I even neglected my health if I saw a way to get ahead in the company. Then one day, when I was thirty-six years old, my wife told me I was a jerk and that she wanted a divorce. At that moment I felt like I woke up, like I didn't know where I'd been for my whole life."

Mike was puttng the pieces together as he spoke, and I listened as his therapist. He told how he moved out of the house, how his marriage ended, and how the children stayed with their mother; the shock of all these changes awakened him to the narrowness of his "successful" life. Starting then, he entered a new phase in his life. Feeling the grief and loss of what happened opened his eyes and led him to a new vitality and excitement. It ignited a fire within him to live his life more fully, to learn how to live a healthy life, and to become all the man he could be.

Life's eye-opening experiences usually happen in ways we don't plan or control. They are often brought by crisis or tragedy. Ultimately, they have the potential to launch us on a path of personal recovery.

Eye-opening Experiences

Adult life inevitably brings experiences that wake us up. No one escapes them. For each man it's different. For some it happens in the loss of a job, the sudden death of a parent, or the serious illness of a child. The jolt comes to some through something wonderful like finding a loving relationship, or the birth of a child. For others it happens after making a major mistake, facing an illness like alcoholism or cancer, or having a car accident.

Every man has his own variation on the theme of adult eye-opening experiences. When it happens, all reality as he knows it shifts like an earthquake reshaping the landscape. Small, everyday events are seen in a totally different light. Problems are viewed with a different perspective. Suddenly, a large bill for a car repair may be seen from a life and death perspective. Now, a man may even feel lucky to be alive to pay it. From this new perspective, it no longer seems worth fretting over.

Men are awakening to new possibilities for coping with crisis by joining self-help groups and recovery programs like Alcoholics Anonymous, Al-Anon, and the many other programs based on the Twelve Steps of Alcoholics Anonymous. Some men are forming support groups or going to workshops to talk about their experiences with other men. They are showing up at post-divorce groups and grief recovery groups, at Parents Without Partners and Suicide Survivors groups. Many therapists report a marked increase in numbers of men in therapy, up from 10 percent of their total caseloads to 30 to

50 percent. Barbara Sullivan, writing in the *Chicago Tribune*, noted that fifteen or twenty years ago,

> Men were expected to take care of their own problems; to ask for professional help was a definite sign of weakness. But ... therapy for men is losing its stigma. Maybe their fathers would have never sat down in front of a therapist's desk, but today's generation of men is more open to the idea.[1]

The women's movement has shed much light and also created a lot of pressure for change in men. Women have taken the initiative in raising gender consciousness as part of personal growth. Men are now also discovering its importance in their lives.

As a family therapist, I see the awakening in my male clients. I also see it in my friends and in the current books about men's issues. Men are saying, "I've been missing something. I love life and I want it as fully as I can have it. I don't want just the narrow slice of life that my dad had. I want to be all the man and all the human being I can be."

But a man can't carry out those changes on his own. The *choice* to change and grow is his alone. But, once that choice is made, regardless of how strong his motivation, the decision will not force his recovery to happen. How to change must be learned. It is learned from the wisdom of others and from the lessons gleaned through life experience — and it takes time.

Catching Fire

This book is about men who survived life crises and how, in the aftermath, their spirit caught fire with a passion for a better way to live. It's about their inner peace and self-confidence, their dedication to living more joyfully than before, and it's about the paths they walk daily to continue to learn and maintain a recovery lifestyle. The bedrock idea of men in recovery comes from men's experiences in dealing with addiction or codependency. But this book is for all men recovering from a life crisis.

This is a book about the spiritual aspects of healthy masculinity — how men learn to feel good about themselves, how they stay emotionally alive and open to new experiences, fulfilling themselves and staying true to their values. It's about confronting themselves with truths that sometimes hurt. It's about exploring the dark and painful corners of their souls and then awakening to new possibilities.

The Struggle to Grow

None of us are completely developed people when we reach adulthood. We weren't complete when we graduated from high school, when we had our first sexual experience, or when we got our first job or our first apartment. When we stay open and alert, life continues to teach us until we die. Often the most painful experiences carry the most valuable lessons. But we also learn from the little details in our lives, the string of mundane mornings when we must get up and go to work, even though we'd rather sleep. We learn from an angry friend when he points out that we neglected to call for three months. And we learn from those we live with as we mutually work out ways to take care of our basic needs like fixing dinner and sweeping the floor.

Not everyone stays open and alert. Not everyone continues to learn and grow in adulthood. The painful experiences come to everyone who lives long enough, but many men shut down emotionally, or they fall into a stupor and miss life's lessons. They may stray from the path of natural adult development onto a dead-end path where they remain emotionally and spiritually asleep for years. Lessons come their way too, but they remain unable to learn from them and insensitive to the messages they carry.

"Who's on Top?"

Mike, the man who suddenly woke up at age thirty-six, had lived with a single answer to his life. It was simply, "Competition and hard work will make you a winner every time." That was his central ethic, his answer to every problem, and his only wisdom. When a problem arose, he pulled together all his willpower, and he heroically tried to conquer it. When someone made a comment, he always tried to top it. He compulsively accepted every challenge without a thought that he could let it go by. He was always a strong competitor, and in his work world it made him a high achiever. He was asleep to nearly every choice of response to life except competition.

Mike was also a strong competitor in his marriage, which didn't work well in an intimate relationship. He could not be emotionally intimate with his wife when his main response to her was competitive. To him, every exchange with her asked the question, "Who's on top?" Anytime she was helpful to him, or she knew something he didn't, or she insisted on her plan, he became vaguely uneasy and felt inadequate. So, as they sat across from each other at their kitchen table, he could never let go and enjoy her company and be playful. Nor could he ask openly for her help when he needed it. He could not simply listen when she expressed her feelings, because he had to fix the situation and give her answers. With his children, he could not relax and just be a good father, because he worried that his wife was a better parent.

Mike's single-solution approach meant that being in the presence of another man automatically forced a contest, a friendly one at times but always a contest. Because competition was his only solution, he was asleep to new learning. He felt he had the answer, but in his slumber he lived in a poverty of spirit. He was unaware of what was missing in his life, unaware of how brittle his strength was or how vulnerable he was to the normal crises of adult life. His fixed and narrow understanding about how to live made him susceptible to the problems of addiction, codependency, physical illness, and relationship difficulties.

He grew up as a child in a troubled family. His father lived in a wheelchair and barked out angry orders to everyone in the family. Mike's greatest wish as a boy was to please his dad, and competition brought that glint of pleasure to his dad's eyes. So amidst pain and chaos, he settled on success as a lifestyle, like a child in danger of drowning who reaches for a floating stick.

At thirty-six, he wasn't growing anymore because he had settled on this narrow answer: *always compete.* It always brought relief from pain and stress before, and it was all he knew. The day his wife finally blurted out her anger and the divorce that followed were painful blows to him. He lost weight; he couldn't sleep at night; he had mood swings ranging from deep depression to complete satisfaction. He was at the place many men reach where only a painful event can get his attention and profoundly shift his perspective. Some lessons we will learn only when we can find no more ways to avoid them. Then, only the intense jolt of crisis will open our eyes.

Many Ways to Stay Asleep, Many Ways to Wake Up

We are each incomplete in our own way. We never arrive at a final point of finished development, until we die. If we aren't growing, we're becoming stagnant. I remind myself of that when I get overcritical about a mistake I've made. Perhaps on the day I finally have learned everything I need to learn and have a grasp on what life is about, I might be ready to die. But for now, I still need to accept my mistakes and keep learning.

It's not important that I make mistakes or that I can't do things perfectly. The important question is, *Am I growing and learning?* Too often a man becomes an underachiever in living. He adds a year to his life with every birthday, but he's only getting older. He doesn't benefit from age, so he only feels bad about it. He doesn't become wiser, or more well-rounded, or more able to love others. He has closed off his learning by settling too early on easy or single answers.

The important questions for a man's development and strength are not, *Am I successful?* or *Am I happy?* Success and happiness come and go throughout life like waves at sea. Sometimes life is easy, and sometimes it is hard. When a man has just one answer to deal with all of life's experiences, he gets narrow and dependent on it. A man who turns to alcohol or other drugs to cope is using that single answer and to avoid his life's lessons. But that is not only true for an addict. It is equally true for the man who only knows how to be aggressive, never submissive, or only knows how to be cool and rational, never following his intuition and feelings. He becomes like the dinosaurs who could deal with a specific set of conditions but couldn't adapt when change occurred.

I've seen an endless variety of crises in men's and women's lives in my career as a marriage and family therapist. Their crises have sometimes frightened me, sometimes taught me about life, and usually created a special relationship with me as their guide. The close contact of personal relationships is the biggest reward of my work. Every person brings a different story and another way of struggling with life. Some problems reach crisis proportions because a person was asleep to the smaller day-to-day messages calling for attention in his life. Others occurred simply at random, like the brick that fell just as you walked by a tall building.

Whatever the story or problem, no matter how different or shocking, whether it seems deserved or undeserved, I always feel I'm getting another glimpse of what it is to be human. I always feel that if my circumstances were reversed with my clients' circumstances, their stories could be mine. I have been privileged to walk closely with people through thousands of crises, and I've been able to learn from them. Their experiences have blended in my mind with the crises in my life and propelled me into my own eye-opening experiences.

A Summer of Growth

One such time in my life happened during a painful summer several years ago. My wife, Mavis, and I knew that her grandmother was old and ill and getting ready to die. I was also painfully aware that the director of the small psychiatric clinic where I worked was seriously ill with cancer. We were emotionally getting ready for these deaths, but we weren't ready for the telephone call that woke us from our sleep early on Memorial Day weekend.

The neighbor of Mavis' parents was calling her to come home immediately. Her father was gravely ill with an unexpected heart attack. She was on the plane within two hours, but she didn't get there in time to say good-bye to him. We had anticipated death, but not the one we faced. Then, on the Fourth of July, my clinic director died a sad and painful death at a young age. On Labor Day weekend the twelve-year-old daughter of our friend was struck and killed by a car as she rode her bicycle across the street.

When that autumn arrived, Mavis' grandmother was still with us, but her son, my father-in-law, was dead. I had said good-bye to my boss and grieved his death, but who could have known a spirited young girl was also to die? Death had scrambled my thoughts. It came where it was expected and where it was not. It came to the very young but not to the very old. Life seemed out of order.

In the heaviness of grief, my perspective was permanently altered in ways that can't quite be captured by words. My eyes were opened to truths about life that surprised me because, in the midst of loss, I felt deeply joyful to be alive. On a quiet Sunday morning that October, I remember riding my bicycle down the street with my daughter in the child's seat behind me, smelling the fresh morning air and feeling reawakened to simple pleasures.

With hindsight, our expectations about who was going to live or die seemed arrogant. We had a new, sharp awareness that mortality is real every moment we live, not just at the end of life, and that a life, no matter how long or short, is a whole life. That summer profoundly changed my outlook on all my activities. I felt it when I stood at the sink scraping carrots and their intense orange color became an occasion to appreciate the beauty of life. When my daughter spilled ink on her new jeans I thought, *What difference does a little stained fabric make when I think of our friends who lost their daughter?* Then I reassured her and myself with a hug.

Crying "Uncle"

People almost always enter therapy because of some crisis. Few of us take on the burden of change until we run out of choices. We may think, *Someday I might go into therapy, someday I'd like to talk this over with a therapist.* But we rarely take the step to invest our time, money, or ourselves in the work until we are pushed by crisis. So, as a therapist, I've quite naturally become a student of crises. I'm interested in what causes problems in people's lives, what they have control over and what they don't, and who will use pain for growth or who just grows another year older.

Some men live with a crisis simmering on the back burner from one year to the next, and they never come to terms with it. They feel successful if they don't have to yield to deal with it. It might be an unresolved relationship problem with a father, a recurring self-esteem problem, or a marriage that is constantly unsatisfactory. These men can't find any options to effectively deal with the problem, so they become numb to it. They carry on until it gets bad enough to boil over into a crisis. Some men are so good at controlling the uproar around them that they can handle the surface effects of problems, but the underlying difficulties go on for years, unresolved and creating tension because they are never acknowledged.

Once problems come to a head, men deal with them in various ways. Some approach problems with a new spirit of life and energy for new learning. Others approach problems with a diehard loyalty to old answers they learned as children. These answers are often inflexible, and no longer adequate for current situations. Some men carry long-established attitudes of defeat and passivity, and a new problem musters only more of the same victim-like attitudes.

It's too bad that people have problems, but "life is trouble," as Zorba the Greek asserts in the novel by Nikos Kazantzakis. Facing problems, and getting help to make changes, is progress. The men I feel most sad for are those who live in chronic stress, always able to hold on tighter, to cope, to smooth it over and carry on, and never crashing, never reaching the point of crisis where they finally cry "uncle." I feel sad for them because they never open up to the possibility of help and a refreshing change.

Beginning Recovery

The very idea of recovery for men is a dubious concept in the minds of some people. They say men are hopeless, genetically or constitutionally incapable of decent human relationships. One woman I know said she had been badly treated and abused too many times by men. She gave up hope for them entirely and said, "Recovery for men? Forget it! Toss them in jail and throw away the key!" Most women are much less bitter, but they are often frustrated in their search for a good male partner, and they ask, "Why are all the men I meet so insensitive, so unfeeling, and immature?" One night, in talking about relationships between the sexes, a male friend said in a hushed, confidential tone, "Merle, when I see how some men act and talk, I'm embarrassed for my gender. I wonder if there is any hope for some men."

Many people say the word "recovery" is a bad one to use because it implies that something is wrong that needs repair. It implies an illness and, by its very image, demeans and shames people. I disagree. "Recovery" is a good word to use because it acknowledges the imperfection of human development. It acknowledges that there are forces acting to undermine and deter our growth. It implies that things can and do go awry, and it also implies the hope that comes when we choose new directions. In using the term *recovery*, I'm talking about all the things adult men have to recover from to continue to grow and learn. We have to recover from addiction and from abusive patterns of relating to others and to ourselves. We also have to recover from the abuses we've suffered, from our insensitivities to women, from our losses and griefs, and from the many ways we didn't get enough or didn't learn enough as children.

The Same Old Coping Response
Produces the Same Old Result

All people facing a life crisis are called upon to respond to their problem with something new from within — perhaps from an inner resource they never used before. The same old coping response either doesn't fit the new reality or it might be exactly what led to the current problem. A man in crisis needs to find new ways to respond that he never knew about — ways of responding and capacities of self that may have lain dormant, undeveloped. He needs a crash course on how to respond differently. He can either let down his guard and become more flexible to learn a new response, or he can hold on rigidly, relying exclusively on old learning and becoming more cemented in old ways.

"The best definition of craziness is . . ."

One man called me for a therapy appointment six weeks after his wife moved out. Through seven years of marriage, he always got what he wanted from her through manipulation. But she gradually grew deeply depressed over the years as she became more emotionally drained by his manipulation. The relationship had the same circular pattern as long as they knew each other. As long as she was attentive and generous, the marriage stayed smooth, but during this phase of the cycle he was cool and inattentive. Eventually, she would get discouraged and pull back or get angry. That would reactivate his attention to her. He would begin making promises and turn on his charm. Then, she would feel hopeful about their marriage and become warm and giving, and he would gradually settle back into his cool, inattentive ways. His persuasive charms brought her back into the relationship hundreds of times before. But now she wouldn't come back again because making up never led to any real change.

He had tried the same seductive response for six weeks. It was the only way he had ever learned to get close to a woman. He was hoping his efforts would produce the same result as they always had, except this time his wife was too depressed to accept it again. He continued to try the only answers he knew — sweet talk, promises, persuasion, and charm. When he called me, he hoped that I could shore up his coping methods, that I would influence his wife to come back.

As one friend once said, "The best definition of craziness is applying the same solution to the same problem over and over again even though it always produces the same disastrous results." If I had directly joined him in his effort to bring his wife back, more of the same response would have only continued the problem cycle in his relationship with her. Instead, we began therapy by directing his attention to himself and what he had learned about intimacy. Our goal was to use his crisis to break free of those old patterns and learn healthier coping responses. In this way, he could become a better partner and feel better about himself.

Male Ways of Falling Asleep and Obstacles to Waking Up

Men in our culture seem to have unique ways of falling asleep and unique hurdles that prevent them from waking up. It isn't maleness that complicates their problems or blocks recovery. It's often narrow options for dealing with life, stalled development, and perceptions of adult masculinity. The forces in our culture that create racism, sexism, materialism, drug and chemical orientation, and militarism are negative influences on every individual's self-esteem and can work against achievement of full human development. These dehumanizing forces tend to make men feel more like objects than thinking and feeling human beings. They create emotions of being only a paycheck to their families, only an employee number on the job, only a body that needs to be worked out and dieted, only a sexual animal with a penis that has a mind of its own, and only a meaningless cog on a wheel. These insidious forces keep men feeling that something is wrong with them, that they are weak and incomplete.

As an illustration, let's look at the developmental level of a thirteen-year-old boy. Thirteen year olds have simple, and often rigidly held, recipe-like ideas about many things, including what it is to be a man. That's normal for that age. They aren't adults yet, but they've been keen observers of fathers and other men in their lives. They notice how their dads act with other men, how they act around women, the swagger in their walk, their posture when they sit, the words they say, and how they say them. At thirteen, a boy understands becoming a man mostly from what he sees men do and the qualities men show on the surface.

I saw this played out one afternoon as I rode my bicycle on a trail through a wooded area. I came upon three boys stopped beside the trail. They looked about thirteen, wide-eyed and boyish, puffing cigarettes like beginners. As I rounded the bend, they spoke loudly and brazenly, stringing together the most vulgar words I'd heard in a long time. The boys were practicing their ideas of adulthood by trying on behaviors they had seen adult men use but which are prohibited to boys. It came out as a humorous exaggeration of men.

Mark Twain said that "at the age of twelve a boy starts imitating a man and he just goes on doing that for the rest of his life." Actually, a grown man deepens and matures through his inner knowledge of masculinity as he gains life experiences. He doesn't need to put on the external appearance of manhood after he becomes a man. This difference is like the contrast between hearing about a trip to Mexico and actually going there yourself. Hearing about Mexican habits and culture, you get some idea of what it's like, but your knowledge has no depth until you've experienced it. You don't know all the exceptions to the description or how to apply the information. With wisdom, the grown man is more flexible than the boy, because his knowing comes from his inner experience. He isn't so rigidly attached to superficial rules that define masculine behavior. *It is precisely this knowing and trusting of inner experience that is central to a spiritual life and to a man's recovery.*

Settling Too Early on a Single Answer

But inner knowing doesn't always develop. Trouble presses us to turn inward and look at our experience. In the midst of our difficulties we may ask, *Is there something wrong with me?* But a man may settle too early on a single answer or find easy solutions to a problem. After settling early on a formula for living, he may stop learning and go to sleep psychologically, he may stop looking inward. Drugs often serve that purpose. Ryne Duren, a former pitcher for the New York Yankees, said, "The first time I asked a girl out, I had been drinking, and once the use of alcohol helped me through that, it was destined to help me through a lot of things — the night of the class play, my first open disagreement with my father, my first sexual involvement."[2]

But as we saw in Mike's example, many so called virtues can also become rigidly held "easy" answers. For example, if the male style of being hard-driving and competitive brings great success early in life, a man may adopt the arrogant belief that he knows enough, that he has mastered life's riddles. Then, he certainly falls asleep to all the other learning he still needs for a full life — learning how to let his wife bring him hot tea with lemon when he's home in bed with the flu; how to tell a trusted friend he's afraid he can't pay all his bills this month; how to visit a desperately ill friend in the hospital; or how to enjoy a walk through the grass, feeling the leaves brush against his feet.

"What more was there to learn?"

Phil was a quarterback on his high school football team. His name was in the local paper every week during fall. Every student in his class knew and admired him. He could date any girl he chose and believed he had the answers to life. What more was there to learn? But when he took off his graduation cap and gown, he entered a world that bewildered him. He got to college and no one knew him. He didn't know how to start a conversation with a stranger or how to feel comfortable in a group when he was just "one of the gang." His high school fame made him think he knew all he needed to know, and he now felt betrayed. He started to rely on alcohol to relax, and he turned bitter about the emptiness he felt at college. The result was a serious crisis because his formula for high school success wasn't the complete formula for his life.

Overcontrol of Feelings

There is tremendous pressure on men and boys to control their feelings. Columnist Russell Baker says that in his boyhood there were "Three absolute requirements . . . to qualify for 'man' status." They were utter fearlessness, a zest for combat, and an indifference to pain.[3] A man's self-esteem may get tied to and distorted by how well he controls his feelings.

"But how did you feel?"

One day I met with a man and woman who came into therapy for help with their new relationship. He had two previous marriages, and now they were worried that they could not sustain a close relationship with each other. During the session the woman told him, "Your thoughtfulness in looking after me while I was in bed with a cold made me grateful to have you in my life." His face turned soft and his eyes moistened. Then I asked him to say what he felt, and he gave a logical, abrupt response, "Well somebody needed to pitch in. That was obvious." His reply was far removed from that soft look in his eyes, so I repeated, "But how do you *feel*?" He became more aware of his real feelings and said, "I don't want to say anymore now because I'm afraid I'll cry." I challenged him by saying, "You can never be close to a woman until you can show your feelings when you feel them."

He is like so many boys and men who were punished or are ridiculed for showing their feelings and their vulnerability. By simple conditioning, they came to feel ugly or unacceptable, as if they deserve rejection when they show feelings. I've often seen men who simply don't know that the majority of women feel more attracted to them, more loving toward them, when they show their feelings. Because many men have associated openness about softer feelings with punishment and shame, they feel repugnant and expect rejection when they show that side. They have an unconscious barrier against ever getting close.

Some men discover that every difficult learning situation, every tense social occasion, and every worry can be calmed by medicating themselves with alcohol or other drugs, work, sex, money, exercise, or food. They can easily gain a *sense* of wellness, a *feeling* of control by merely lifting a glass, swallowing a pill, rushing into the excitement of a new romance or fleeting sexual encounter, or going on a food or spending binge. The single-answer feeling of control puts men asleep to further adult learning. It keeps them out of touch with their inner voice and stalls their learning at a thirteen-year-old's level. Then, only the shock of crisis has the possibility of reigniting their fire. A truly healthy, hopeful, and optimistic life requires us to walk through the tension of learning unfamiliar and sometimes uncomfortable lessons, rather than numbing our insecurities with drugs, sex, or work.

How Men Use Therapy

Men are much more likely than women to enter the growth experience of therapy with an operational approach. They ask me to spell out and clearly state the goals for their therapy. They want to know the rational explanations for things and they look for a step-by-step procedure that they expect will lead them to a known outcome. Many men are not well-acquainted with the intuitive aspects of human learning and the uses of symbol and metaphor. When I challenge them to expand their thinking, their first reaction is to mistrust my approach rather than to recognize that they're encountering a gap in their learning. They sometimes imply that I'm not hard-headed enough. Until they learn more about their own intuitive powers, these men believe everything can be consciously thought out, weighed, categorized, and determined.

Hope for Men's Recovery

When I think about the question of hope for men's recovery, I remember a talk I heard by the famous psychologist, Rollo May. He spoke on the spiritual issues in personal growth, and someone in the audience asked if he believed in resurrection. As I recall, May answered that he didn't know about life after death, but he saw resurrections take place every day with his clients right in his office, several on a good day! It's been true for me, for several friends, and for scores of clients. When a sleeping man wakes up, he catches fire with the spirit of new possibilities for his life.

EXERCISES FOR EYE OPENING

Here are exercises that can help you take the ideas in this chapter and apply them to your life. Use the ones that seem helpful and modify them to fit your needs.

- Make a list of all the shocks and crises you have had in your life. Write the list as fast as you can, perhaps giving yourself five minutes to list as many as you can, including both big and small ones. When the five minutes are up, go back and reflect on two or three of the events. What did you learn from them? Which events are you recovering from today? Which ones contributed to growth earlier in your life? How did you use the experience to grow?

- Did you settle on answers to life that you later learned were not sufficient? What were they? Were they ideas about lifestyle? Morality? Career? Religion? Friendships? Marriage?
- What beliefs do you hold now about how a healthy man should live and act? Can you trace a path back to where you learned to believe these things?
- Virginia Satir explained, "The most hope-producing, self-esteem-lifting experience we can have is to hear and be heard by another person." To gain hope and deepen your learning for your own recovery, tell another man your story as it came to mind while you read this chapter. If he is also willing to talk about himself, listen to his story.

CHAPTER 2

Finding Your Inner Warrior: Learning the Wisdom of Surrender

Are you willing to be sponged out, erased,
cancelled, made nothing?
Are you willing to be made nothing?
dipped into oblivion?
If not you will never really change.
— *D.H. Lawrence*

The one thing expected of the stereotypical "good man" in our culture is a healthy strain of toughness and strength. We teach our young boys to be little soldiers or little cowboys. We overemphasize one good side of masculinity and teach boys to be strong, to never give in, to be number one. When they get hurt we coach them to "take it like a man," which means don't flinch and don't show feelings. We want our boys to become dominant, aggressive go-getters and not to need anybody. The late Vince Lombardi, the Green Bay Packers' football coach, expressed this one-sided view for many men with his classic quip, "Winning isn't everything, it's the only thing."

Surrender Is a Healthy Life Skill

Most dictionary definitions of the word *surrender* have a negative tone. The *Oxford American Dictionary* defines it as: "to hand over, to give into another person's power or control" or, "to give oneself up, to accept an enemy's demand for submission." *Webster's* lists one definition of *surrender* as "to yield or resign oneself to an emotion, influence, etc."

But surrender is a positive factor in the rhythm of change and renewal. It's a valuable, often crucial coping method, which sometimes literally means the difference between life and death. It's a way to allow healing to begin, a way to go forward from a problem that seems impossible to get beyond, a way to let go of the past, and a way to get close to others.

Still, surrender has been a big stumbling block for men. In the way we understood masculinity, surrender felt shameful. It seemed like a violation of ourselves. We are supposed to be good soldiers and for a soldier, surrender is not often an option. Yet, to yield, to surrender, is actually another form of strength in many situations. It is part of being a good team member to submit your individual talents to the team effort. It's part of being a successful student to submit to the authority and knowledge of your teacher. It's part of being a good father to growing children to submit to their increasing need for independence and separateness. It's part of a respectful relationship to yield sometimes to your mate's wishes. It's part of a fulfilling sexual experience to surrender to your feelings. Surrender is even a necessary part of the simple process of falling asleep at night.

A man in a burning house who only knows how to stay and fight to the bitter end is in danger of dying in the flames. If he retreats or gets help, he might survive, even if he loses something to the flames. Experts on stress tell us that the fact of stress in our lives is not usually a problem: stress within limits is normal. The problem comes when we operate constantly at a high-stress level, never letting down, never yielding to relaxation, never venting our feelings. Surrender in the form of a night's rest, taking time to play with friends, celebrating, or talking about our feelings, is part of a rhythm that restores our strength, our physical immunity, and our inner resources before we return to the stressful situation.

Men and Surrender

In other cultures and other times, men have learned to use surrender as a way to live a better life. The Zen master Shunryu Suzuki, for example, taught his followers to practice a "beginner's mind" as a way to stay open to life's lessons. We are used to seeking control and thinking it's better to look knowledgeable. Some people are so ashamed of being a beginner and looking "ridiculous" that they never try anything new. Shunryu Suzuki taught his students the beginner's attitude as a way of life, saying it is wise for all people because it keeps them ready to learn. He said, "In the beginner's mind there are many possibilities, in the expert's mind there are few."[1]

On the temple of Apollo at Delphi, Greece, the admonition, "Know Thyself," was inscribed twenty-five hundred years ago. Following that guidance, Greek men would surrender to the truth about themselves and become stronger for it. Christ taught, "He that findeth his life shall lose it; and he that loseth his life for My sake shall find it."

Too much submission can be just as lopsided as too much aggression. But it seems today that men are set up for more than their share of life problems when no one teaches them that yielding is an aspect of wisdom and strength. Men don't have to stop being assertive. They just need to add the ability to yield with self-respect; to tune in to their inner voices and to accept the message in their circumstances.

As men, we specialize in varieties of toughness, strength, and power. Having a muscular body is only one form of strength. We also admire a tough-minded man who has a "take-charge attitude"; we admire an executive who is aggressive. We're entertained by our sports heroes when they're tough. "Silent" almost naturally flows from our lips after "strong," as we describe a hero who learned to hold back his feelings. The Lone Ranger was glorified specifically because he didn't need anybody. His loneliness was heroic, and we saw it as a sign of strength.

When a man runs for public office, we expect him to make a point of demonstrating his toughness to us. We saw just how far off-balance this single value had become in the United States when Edmund Muskie ran for president in 1968. In New Hampshire, during a primary election, he cried with feeling in a public appearance, after his wife was criticized. That one moment of human emotion was said to have ruined his chance to be elected president. The worst thing we can do to a man's image is to suggest he isn't strong by calling him a wimp. Avoiding the "wimp" label was George Bush's greatest challenge in his successful run for the presidency.

My Own Experience with Surrender

I had a personal experience with surrender during the days my mother was dying seven years ago. Our family sat every evening beside her hospital bed. We knew there was no hope for her recovery. The doctor told us that enzyme tests showed her heart attack was as massive as he had ever seen. Her heart was enlarged to the size of a football. She was in no pain, just incredibly weak and getting weaker. So, every day was possibly the last opportunity to talk with her, to tell her the small details of my life that day, to tell her again that I loved her, and to hear her say it back; then to say good night again. She felt a peaceful acceptance of God's will for her. She could accept death, but she loved life. Death was clearly not her choice.

These final days were strung like beads on a strand, day after day, and then week upon week. My worry about her death slowly and ironically changed to worry that she might live, imprisoned by life as a chronic invalid. At 5:30 one morning, my brother called me to the hospital. We sat with her, held her hand, and talked to her. The mood was intense, and my brain was involuntarily scanning the possibilities for escape. I felt the impulse to run out of the room. I wanted her to die quickly now to get past this pain. I felt a sudden surge of anger at the whole situation. My dad came into the room and walked out again many times. My sister, brother, and sister-in-law sat for a while with Dad in the lounge, and I was alone with Mom. Her breathing grew more labored and I paced around her bed. If I left she would be totally alone, but I couldn't control my nervous energy and sit still.

Then the nurse came in, checked her vital signs and said to me in a calm, quiet voice, "I don't think it will be much longer. Why don't you just sit down beside her? Hold her hand and tell her you're here." She walked out again, closed the door, and graciously left us alone. I was relieved to surrender to her suggestion, relieved I didn't have to sift through the storm of feelings and impulses in my brain for a decision about what to do. I calmly sat beside her bed and held her hand. Mother gasped for air, her throat rattled, her chest heaved as she desperately reached for one more moment of life. I talked to her through the tears falling down my cheeks. "Mom, we're here with you. We love you. God loves you." And I said it again and again, forcing the words out of my throat. My brother returned to the room and he talked to her. I put my face closer to her ear so she could hear me above the sound of her own breath, but she could not respond because she was totally consumed by her last fight.

I had thought, somehow, that when the final moment came, she would quietly, peacefully slip away. Suddenly, her heart would just stop beating. But her battle to hold on to life was like the last sprint of a long-distance runner who wrings out every remaining ounce of energy for the last few yards of the race. She fiercely tried to breathe, to get more air. The sounds she made were not the quiet, passive moans I expected from my tired, weak mom. She made powerful, shuddering groans and gasps until she crossed the final marker and literally no life was left in her.

My emotional defenses had been softened during that month-long string of last days and last good-byes. Then, they were absolutely stripped away on my last morning with her. I was like a child in wonderment. I was no longer aloof. I was no longer a detached observer inside my ego defenses, evaluating, intellectualizing, minimizing. The little details of my life, the meaning of things, were all rearranged. I didn't decide to change. It happened to me! I had been transformed. During the ensuing weeks, friends came to me, and, as we talked about our feelings and their feelings, I was always easily touched and warmed. I cried shamelessly and talked more openly and honestly than I ever had before. I was far beyond trying to control my emotions, and it felt right. I thought to myself how strange it was in the midst of our sad loss to feel something very healing. How good it felt to not be self-conscious, to not fight it, but to surrender.

Unconscious Loyalty to the "Strong Man"

We men sometimes don't know how to say "uncle" when it is time to surrender. Most of us don't realize how loyal we are to the image of the "Strong Man." I wasn't aware of how attached I was to it until I was well into my thirties. After all, I didn't believe in violence, and I always tried to be considerate and sensitive toward others. But I certainly did think that the more independent and self-sufficient I was, the better man I would be. When I didn't have to ask for help, I felt proud. When I kept my feelings contained I was more satisfied with myself. I have since learned that my idea of self-esteem was shallow. I discovered that this one-sided form of development leaves out the spiritual aspects of masculinity. It leaves men stranded in perpetual adolescence because they do not learn valuable lessons about self-image that go beyond the beginning stages of masculine development. Those valuable lessons are learned by developing a relationship with our inner warrior. The inner warrior knows that life is difficult. He knows that sometimes moving with a blow is better than resisting it. He knows that the bottom line is not always "Who won?" but, "Do I respect myself for how I played?"

We have very few popular models today of men who have grown beyond youthful muscle-flexing to become deeper, wiser, more whole men. Instead, many mornings we read that another public figure or sports hero wound up in jail for drunken driving, or even worse, died of a drug overdose. We see an intense pursuit of a quick fix for problems, seeking the better drug to control our moods, lusting for the most money at the earliest possible time, longing for the most powerful car to drive.

Many Men Are Trapped

As a result of this stagnation in developing our ideals, we have to face adult challenges with learning and wisdom more suited to a teenager. And in our private moments, when we listen carefully to our feelings, we find a gnawing emptiness. We feel lost, cut off from ourselves and others, and somehow defective. We wonder, *What's missing? Is something wrong with me? Is this all there is?*

Surrender and receptiveness are ways to love and connect with the people and the world around us. Without that skill we feel oppressed, stifled, and isolated. We may always feel on display, even to ourselves, always self-conscious, tense and concerned about how well we're doing. We can't forget ourselves because we feel too vulnerable, so we stay trapped and unchanging in self-centeredness.

Unable to surrender, the only way to get beyond ourselves, to get back to a sense of excitement and a breath of fresh air, is to be overwhelmed by forces more powerful than our walls of resistance. These forces may come from either within or outside ourselves.

How a powerful drug or alcohol affects us is a good example for showing how these forces work. Taking a drink or shooting up, a man doesn't have to learn how to surrender, to relax, or to let down. He doesn't have to go through the difficult process of struggling with awkwardness and mistakes. Instead, he retains the illusion of control by using the drug to get the predictable result, just as he might press a switch to flick on the lights. The drug relaxes him while he holds as tightly as ever to his willfulness. He temporarily forgets himself and escapes the trap of self-obsession. It feels like a wonderful experience, a well-deserved relief.

Glen Gray writes about the "appeals of battle" for men who, through the pain and ugliness of war, have ecstatic experiences. The intensity of battle acts like a drug they lose themselves in.

> The threat to life and safety that the presence of the opponent, "the enemy," represented created this climate of feeling. Near the front it was impossible to ignore, consciously or unconsciously, the stark

fact that out there were men who would gladly kill you, if and when they got the chance. As a consequence, an individual was dependent on others, on people who could not formerly have entered the periphery of his consciousness.[2]

Elsewhere in his book he writes of the intensity of battle: "We feel rescued from the emptiness within us. In losing ourselves we gain a relationship to something greater than the self, and the foreign character of the surrounding world is drastically reduced."[3] Gray even uses the ideas of surrender and transformation when he says that a soldier who gets high on battle "has yielded himself to the fortunes of war" and that "he must surrender in a measure to the will of others and to superior force," and as a result, "is no longer what he was."[4]

It is a sad truth that the force of gruesome battle conditions may be the only way to overwhelm some men's soldier/cowboy defenses.

This same overwhelming experience with the same addictive potential comes to many men through sexual excitement, drinking or drug use, eating, sports and physical conditioning, anger outbursts, physical abuse, shoplifting, or gambling. When a "good American boy," holding to his "never-give-in" and "don't-admit-your-feelings" attitudes happens upon one of these ways of self-forgetting, he may return to it again and again, and he is vulnerable to becoming fully addicted to these behaviors.

Dropping Soldier/Cowboy Defenses

Change is the only constant. Many changes waiting in the wings of life are difficult, painful, or enemies of our health, our loved one's safety, and our peace and security. Life constantly has a difficult and a dangerous side for human beings. We don't need to live in constant fear of change, but to act like we are invulnerable or unmoved is to live in a state of denial. Regardless of how safe we feel at one moment, how much we feel like winners in the game of life, how much we try to reach the top of the heap or think we are untouchable, we are, in fact, each part of a human community that is constantly changing. Enemies don't only exist on the battlefield, though they may be more clear there. We are bonded to all people by the fact that we have enemies around us and within us that threaten our safety and security at all times.

Perhaps there is a balance between anxiously focusing on the dangers around us at one extreme, and total denial of reality at the other. I think a man finds this balance through his relationship with his inner warrior. That warrior has the street smarts to know he is surrounded by dangers and the spiritual knowledge to know that he does not have to deal with the dangers all alone. He has the courage to live life as much more than a battle experience. We share the dangers and trials of life with all people. We all live on the edge. Once the soldier/cowboy denial is dropped and we face these facts, we are less vulnerable to the seductions of destructive intense experiences. After we admit we are living on the edge, that we are in the same boat with all people, we don't require a bigger-than-life experience to excite or impress us and overwhelm our defenses.

The Wisdom of Surrender

The emotionally mature strong man is in touch with the warrior within and knows the wisdom of yielding. A man who doesn't know how to yield lacks the receptive traits of masculine self-esteem. The inner warrior is receptive when he cooperates rather than dominates; when he accepts people as they are rather than trying to change them; when he is playful rather than goal oriented; when he listens and absorbs rather than persuades; when he reflects rather than acts. When a man without the wisdom óf surrender yields, cooperates, or gives in to a partner or friend, he feels bad about himself for having done it. He feels defeated or humiliated. Because of the narrowness such a man grew up with, his feelings of masculinity are locked exclusively into actions of power and dominance. His self-esteem survives only until he meets a situation that he cannot conquer.

There are many versions of this often-heard formula: set your objectives, plan your course of action, work hard, take charge, and you'll reach your goal. This formula is good for getting a job done, but it doesn't apply to the goal of healing and recovery. Listening to the inner voice, to intuition, and reflecting on the silent meaning in an unexpected event are traits of many wise men throughout history.

I've noticed a difference between those men who grew wiser as a result of life crises and those who were destroyed by them. Those who used their life experience for learning, who used surrender as a new opening for possibilities in their lives, and who stopped beating up on themselves for their failures, tended to get better. Out of their weakness grew strength. These men tell about a deeper understanding and appreciation for life as a result of their crises. Through painful, frightening days of new honesty and self-doubt, they found new options. They developed the freedom to give in, to learn from their experiences, to let go of impossible situations, and to move forward. I don't mean they became passive, limp dishrags when the going got rough, only that they now had two capacities instead of one: to try hard, and to yield. It made them stronger than ever to have the option of surrender in coping with their lives.

A Lesson in Rock Climbing

In rock climbing, although I'm safely tied to ropes in case I fall, I naturally try desperately to hold on when making a hard move. I struggle and sweat to get past the difficulty. But, if I slip off the hold and fall, perhaps swinging on the rope to a slightly different place on the rock, I suddenly find new holds and new possibilities for moving up that weren't available at my previous spot.

The Greatest Barrier to Recovery

Many observers see men's resistance to surrender as the greatest stumbling block to recovery. Russell Baker describes a male outlook that "sprang from the fact that in perilous times a man may be required by his country to face death in battle. To fulfill that duty, it helps if early in life you have been taught that being a man often requires conduct that is neither sensible nor natural, but is nevertheless honorable."[5]

Phyllis Silverman works with men who have suffered the shock of their wives' death. She and Scott Campbell say the traditional "machismo" man takes "pride in remaining unaffected by life, in being able to press through with your will in spite of everything." They studied men from age thirty to ninety-four and found that the man who recovers from his grief finds a way to accept it, not to deny it but to take it in. He has "the courage to embrace all the ways that life does affect you, because that means you are alive, and taking pride in your need for others, because that is part of what makes you human."[6]

"You were easier to live with when you had cancer . . ."

One man illustrated for me his father's back-and-forth struggle with surrender. This man had a dreadful relationship with his abusive, alcoholic father. When his father got cancer, the old man suddenly set aside his mean facade of toughness. Facing imminent death, he had the courage to drop his defenses, and he became more honest and vulnerable. He saw his relationship with his son in a new light and realized for the first time that he had been abusive. He openly regretted the beatings he had given his son as a child, and the verbal disrespect he had shown him. He expressed his love and the son welcomed this opportunity for resolution with his father before it was too late.

Then, unexpectedly, the father's cancer went into remission and so did his open, vulnerable attitude. Sadly, as the father felt healthier, he disappeared again behind his mean, defensive barriers. His doctor told him, "Jack, you were emotionally healthier when you were worried about cancer, because then you were easier to live with."

Surrender Is Required

Surrender to reality is an absolute requirement for recovery. Whatever the crisis, in order to make repairs and take your life in a new direction, you have to admit the seriousness of your situation. Many recovering alcoholics have said, "I tried my own ways long enough and they didn't work. My life only got worse. Finally, when I gave in and admitted I needed help, I began to learn something new." As long as we cling to what we believe is "certain," as long as we hold tenaciously to *our* game, we only recycle what we already know.

Warren's Questions for Himself

I have a friend named Warren in the men's recovery group I attend. I always like to listen to him because he has developed a good deal of wisdom over the years of his recovery. One day he told our group that when he checks with himself and wonders, *How am I doing?* he no longer asks *Am I self-reliant?* That used to be his first question, but he quit asking it. He doesn't consider it important to his wellness and strength. Instead, he asks *Am I open to the support, the help, and the new information that comes to me.* This new attitude has made his life much more relaxed. He is now more in contact with reality. He has surrendered and it has made him a more powerful man. And he isn't trying to *prove* his maleness or strength to himself or anyone else. The challenge and the adventure for him now is to continue being open in his relationships with himself, others, and the natural world.

Grieving Our Old Selves

Grief feelings often arise after we let go, after we surrender. Then, we may even wish we could close the opening we made to truth and return to our cocoon. When a client comes in, telling about his sad feelings about his past, and grieving the years he missed by not learning some things sooner, then I'm confident that his changes are deep and genuine.

When genuine change comes, a person may grieve deeply, saying, "If only I had known then what I know now!" Growth challenges us with that pain. A beloved psychologist, John Brantner, said, "The primary task of adult life is to learn how to grieve." Inevitably, we must let go of many of the things we're attached to, including our familiar, unhealthy behaviors.

First we learn to surrender; then we feel the grief that follows; and then we must go even further and surrender to the grief itself rather than beat it back. This is the process of transformation. This is how we work with the mystery of powerlessness and allow change and growth into our lives.

Through this mystery, a new healing occurs, and a feeling of peace, self-acceptance, and excitement comes over us.

Inner Strength through Fear

Fear is another challenge when we surrender. When I let go of my facade of self-sufficiency, I have no guarantee that I will be accepted by those I love. If I'm alcoholic and I agree to never take another drink, where will I turn when I need relief and comfort? Can I survive? If I am in a primary love relationship and pledge to be faithful, can I exist with no door for escape? These can be very frightening questions. The challenge is to live through this fear, to admit that the fear is there, and to hold true to the choice that frightens us. Many of us haven't learned that we can be afraid and still carry on. We can meet the challenge of fear not by running from it, but by turning to face it. It's okay to be afraid. Fear is a useful inner warning system about danger that allows us to stop, be aware, and say, *Sure I'm afraid. Now I'll continue carefully on my course.*

Willpower Versus Acceptance

By making active decisions of *will*, you can get results that you cannot get by an accepting attitude. But the reverse is also true. With an accepting, *receptive mind*, you gain certain benefits that the willful, go-getter attitude cannot bring. You can decide to go fishing, but you can't catch a fish simply through willpower. The more ready you are with an attractive bait, a sharp hook, and an alert mind, the more likely you are to have fish for dinner. Leslie H. Farber wrote a wonderful series of essays on this topic that were published in a book called *Lying, Despair, Jealousy, Envy, Sex, Suicide, Drugs, and the Good Life.*[7]
A man can decide to drive to Chicago and actually go there. He can use his *will* to achieve what he wants. He can set

his goal, get in his car, fill the gas tank, follow the road map, and, with a certain amount of luck, reach his destination. But if he wants to have a warm relationship with his girlfriend on the trip, he can only be ready to do his part, to meet her with a warm spirit. A relationship is within that category of experiences that he can be *open* to, but he can never create it by willful, decisive action.

Unfortunately, we men know best how to be active, decisive, willful, forceful, and we know least how to surrender, to give in, or to be receptive. As a result, we often unwittingly block or fail to notice the experiences we can have only by being receptive. The experienced fisherman knows there are some things he cannot force. His skill is in being ready. If he is too active, moving his line, checking the bait, trying to hook a fish, he may actually drive the fish away.

This distinction between decisive will and open receiving is crucial for men's recovery. We don't have to give up our ability to set goals and take decisive action. But we need to learn additional skills to be open to receive what comes to us. This learning often first begins when we feel defeated, when we surrender to a reality we can no longer ignore, block, or force in the direction we want.

A typical male problem like this sometimes appears clinically as a sexual one. Impotence, when caused by psychological problems, often occurs because a man doesn't know how to surrender to nature. Erections come and go naturally; they are sometimes unpredictable, even for a man who is physically healthy. Research done by Masters and Johnson clearly documents that when we receive sexual stimuli we are aroused. When we are distracted, we may no longer be aroused even if the stimuli are present. The distraction preventing the erection could be leftover tension from work, lack of privacy, anxiety, or negative feelings in the relationship.

A man who only understands how to be decisive during sex may block his sexual pleasure by being personally threatened when his erection goes away. His will is naturally not in full control of his body, but he thinks it should be. He doesn't know about trusting nature and accepting how it works. He may think if he's not in control, he's less of a man. Thus, he tries to force sexual arousal, but arousal doesn't occur by force of will, so he gets worried and feels ashamed. Since he's worried, he is further distracted from sexual stimulation and therefore won't become aroused until he becomes more receptive. He has blocked the natural process with his will; he cannot force an erection to happen. In this way, a man not knowing about acceptance and surrender can extend a normal temporary impotence into a chronic impotence problem that lasts for years because every time he is in a sexual situation, he gets distracted by his fears.

In a recent news article I read, a pilot tried to close the door of his plane after it opened during flight. As I recall the story, a rush of air blew him out of the plane. Miraculously, he was able to grab part of a step outside the door to avoid falling thousands of feet to his death. His co-pilot flew back toward the airport, with the pilot desperately holding on to the outside step, and landed within fifteen minutes. The pilot was saved from disaster and was safely on the ground, but he couldn't release his grasp from the steel bar; his fingers had to be forcibly pried from the step.

It is like that for many of us men when we decide to surrender. After deciding with our rational will to let go, nothing changes until we also learn how to *allow* it to happen.

Learning the Skill of Wise Surrender

We men are so control-oriented most of us know only how to lean in one direction — how to try harder. If our barriers were lower, it would take less stress to overcome them, less intensity to be released from them, perhaps even a lower level of crisis to catch our attention. We would be more accessible to our partners and lovers, and we would more easily feel the awe and mystery of a beautiful moment, or a conversation with a friend. Having lower defenses is something we can learn.

Many spiritual exercises teach the skill of wise surrender. For example, the folklore and spirituality in many American Indian tribes use a gentle trickster to open people to new awareness. This trickster uses stories and experiences that make people laugh, that surprise, frighten, and confuse them into opening their minds to lessons they can't easily learn with a logical approach. The trickster takes people beyond controlled, predictable thinking to feeling and experiencing. Out of it comes new wisdom that could not easily be learned another way.

Carlos Casteneda describes his startling and confounding experiences with a wise native shaman in Mexico, named Don Juan, in a series of books beginning with *The Teachings of Don Juan*. Through numerous surprises, tricks, and confusing experiences, the shaman breaks apart Carlos' common sense beliefs about reality so he can introduce him to deeper truths. They walk long distances together across the desert wilderness in the dark night and hear strange sounds and see strange things. The shaman startles and cajoles Carlos into surrendering his fixed ideas about life and reality so he can become receptive to new learning.

Another spiritual exercise that may be seen as teaching surrender comes from Zen Buddhism. The Zen masters of Japan pose confounding questions called *koans* for their students. A koan doesn't follow usual patterns of logic. One well-known koan asks, "What is the sound of one hand clapping?" Since there is no logical answer to these questions, a student grappling with a koan will try to find a window into deeper truth and to the self. Says Frederick Franck . . . "The koan lets the psyche become a spiritual battlefield, until all the mental resources of the disciple are exhausted. It lets the intellect struggle until it has to give up."[8] Out of surrender comes healing of the inner doubts and conflicts, and awakening to one's true humanness. Daito of Kyoto, Japan, wrote, "Over thirty years I have lived in a fox hole, now I have changed to human status."[9]

A friend of mine says, "Life itself is a Zen master," because in the course of living we are faced with many confusing and surprising situations that have no orderly, logical answers or explanations. The experiences of life are filled with spiritual messages and deeper questions, and we need more than logic to learn how to learn from them.

Out of the Confusion

A man in therapy often experiences confusion. As he confronts and lets go of old, unhealthy attitudes, he may feel dreadfully confused. We all have a set of ideas that act like a compass to give us a feeling of direction. Letting go of those ideas may come when we realize we were abused as children, or when we admit we're addicted, or when we reveal a secret we've never told anyone before, or when we get a divorce. Letting go of one idea of stability leaves us feeling vulnerable until we develop a new one. A client often comes in after an important breakthrough in his therapy, and says, "I feel more upset, more distressed now than ever." The feeling is temporary. Confusion sets the stage for new learning. It is the necessary emptiness that follows letting go of old ideas and makes room for new ones. It's a familiar process to therapists.

Willing to be Surprised

Surrender itself has a very confusing aspect. We are faced with the absolute requirement to surrender and yet, if we only rationally decide to comply, we may in fact still be maintaining control. If we will ourselves to be less willful, we are still using our will. That is like trying to douse a flame by pouring gasoline on it. This is a paradox that can only be resolved by a totally new frame of mind.

One man I know who learned about the need to surrender tried to apply it to his life. He came to my office one day with a bad cold and a runny nose. He said that when he realized he was getting sick he decided not to fight it, but to surrender and go to bed. He complained, "That didn't help either." He thought that surrender was just another formula that produced specific results: "If I give in I'll get better."

But, in true surrender, we are willing to be surprised. We trust that we won't be destroyed, that we have no claim on the outcome. We are committed to learn from whatever happens. Surrender often feels like stepping off a cliff into a free-fall, trusting that where we land will be a starting place for our next growth experience.

Some Native American tribes have a rite of passage they call a vision quest. Men go off alone to fast for several days in search of spiritual growth and insight. In *The Book of the Vision Quest*, Stephen Foster and Meredith Little describe the adaptation of the vision quest for people who live in a modern culture.[10] They go into the wilderness to find a spot where they are alone, but within reach of help if needed. They stay there with only a sheet of plastic for a shelter, and they fast for three days. That time without food, exposed to the elements and alone, creates a vulnerability that may be like the vulnerability people feel in life crisis and in some stages of therapy or treatment for addiction. It can cause people to voluntarily open the door to surrender, so that they can reopen their learning and be more accessible and less defensive with others in their lives.

Sue Serrone describes this experience in the vision quest as crossing a threshold from the mind to the heart. She says it is often a struggle on the vision quest to surrender and move over the threshold. But fasting and aloneness makes people more receptive. Looking at a mountain, the rational mind says, *It's just a mountain.* Seeing a bird or a tree, the rational mind may want to identify them. But during the vision quest, people have less of a buffer between them and their experience, so they are profoundly moved by seemingly small things. The rational point of view retreats while the heart gains prominence. They may perceive the ultimate symmetry in a rock or the friendship that is apparent in the face of a bird when it lands on a nearby branch. The world suddenly seems closer, and people are opened up to their own deep well of experience.[11]

EXERCISES FOR WISE SURRENDER

- Make a list of all the confrontations you can remember in your life. These could be any kind of confrontation that comes to mind, big ones or small ones. Some might be with another person — your father, mother, boss, teacher, wife, friend, child. Or they might be with a challenging situation such as school, an illness, athletics, or any disappointing moment. After making a list, pick three of the confrontations and describe how you dealt with them. Do you find a pattern in how you respond to challenge? What have you learned from your life confrontations? Which ones transformed you? Would they have worked out differently had you chosen to surrender?

- Give someone a gift with no strings attached. Simply think of someone you would like to give a gift to and do it with no expectations in return.

- Tell someone you can trust about a private feeling you have or a dream you had.

- Let someone else's schedule intrude on your own, so you set aside your plans to make room for something you didn't plan. Maybe someone makes a suggestion or invitation you would normally brush aside. Accept it. Or, maybe someone has a need for your help that intrudes on your plans. Give the help.

- Think of ways that you can forget yourself. Is it in going fishing that you leave your cares behind? Is it in playing cards with friends? In the outdoors? In baking bread? In listening to music? Do you have life-giving ways of losing yourself or strength-draining ways? Do you allow yourself what is good for you?

- Make plans for playtime with friends with no goal besides simply having a good time.

CHAPTER 3

Masculine Spirituality: Lighting a Candle in Your Inner World

> *In music, in the sea, in a flower, in a leaf,*
> *in an act of kindness ... I see what people*
> *call God in all these things.*
> — *Pablo Casals*

When a man takes notice of his inner self and trusts it, when he feels a connection with things larger than himself, he has begun his spiritual development. But for many men, it's like they have lived in a house, but only slept there. The interior of their house remains unfamiliar and unexplored. They've been so busy doing, working, and looking outward that they hardly noticed the inner chambers of their own house.

But a change may occur. Perhaps because of a crisis in his life, or because of a painful experience, a man may begin to see everything from a new perspective. As if for the first time, he walks into his neglected, unfamiliar inner world. He lights a candle that sheds light on one small corner, and he begins to peer around and explore this part of his life. It is an experience — not a goal to fulfill, not a job to do, not an idea or a lesson to learn. It is all new to him — strange, but interesting and full of possibilities. This exploration may continue for a lifetime, but having experienced it once — now having cast light into that interior place — his transformation has begun. He will never be the same again.

Marion Woodman, a well-known Jungian analyst and writer, commented in an interview, "At the very point of the vulnerability is where the surrender takes place — that is where the god enters. The god comes in through the wound."[1]

Not Religion

When I talk in this chapter about the spiritual development of recovering men, I'm not talking about religion. People in Alcoholics Anonymous have long known that spirituality and religion are not the same. That insight has become immensely helpful to many people searching for renewal in their lives. The change people undergo in recovery from chemical dependency is called "a spiritual awakening." For many men, even the mention of a spiritual life immediately brings bad memories and a bad taste to their mouth because they associate spirituality with feelings they've had about religious dogma. They were told at one time to follow overly strict or perfectionistic rules that served to condemn them and to stifle their spirits rather than awaken them.

Millions of people find their spiritual life nurtured by a religious faith and practice, but I have also known many highly religious people that didn't seem spiritual at all. These are two distinct, separate qualities. Spirituality is about connections, relationships, and honoring personal experience.

Seeing the World from an Immigrant's Perspective

In 1982 there was a need in our town for a temporary home for a Polish refugee. He arrived from

Poland soon after the Soviets crushed the Solidarity movement there. Our oldest daughter had just gone away to college and we had a room. My wife, our younger daughter, and I talked it over and decided we'd like to have this man as our guest while he was introduced to a new life in Minnesota. My awareness of small details of our life changed the moment we first drove home with him from the airport.

First, we stopped at a restaurant to order lunch. We told our new guest, Joseph, that he could order whatever pleased him. We tried to explain the glossy, colorful menu using our simplest English and talking very slowly. I was suddenly keenly aware of the abundance of our food choices. Pictures I had seen in the newspaper of meat shortages and food lines in Poland rolled through my head while we sat next to him in the booth, describing for him the choices he had of hamburgers, pork chops, or roast beef.

After lunch we drove the few blocks to our tree-shaded, three-bedroom home. Turning into the driveway, I pushed the button above my car's visor to activate our automatic garage door opener. In the midst of this routine motion, my mind stopped momentarily with the awareness of what this must be like for Joseph, who had just escaped his country with little more than his clothing. Everywhere I turned in the days that followed, I tried to see my world from Joseph's perspective. Going to the supermarket with displays of fresh produce piled high, watching the nightly news about citizens publicly criticizing our president, working out at the health club — almost every ordinary routine had a new and heightened impact for me simply because

Joseph was there. I was constantly wondering what each situation, each experience, seemed like to our new friend.

That's how I think of a spiritual awakening as it develops in a growing man. He has a new relationship with life that changes how he sees and feels about everything and everyone.

What Is a Spiritual Relationship?

A spiritual relationship is a connection to something beyond our conscious, decision-making selves. Some call it a relationship to something deep within ourselves. Others call it a relationship with God or with nature. It's about accepting possibilities that can't be proved or measured, and it creates a feeling of aliveness. It means going beyond the "nothing but" perspective of science and technology to attaining a sense of beauty and awe. It means using our personal experience in addition to logic. It means using images, stories, and metaphors, our inner voice, our "gut feeling" as ways to understand our lives.

"I started to acknowledge how many losses I had as a child. . . ."
A man named Andy told me how his relationship grew with a deep, silent part of himself. It began when his life became chaotic after his girlfriend of several years got pregnant. She wanted to get married, but he knew from the bottom of his toes that he could not be a good father or husband. They stayed in the relationship with each other anyway. She had the baby, and the two of them decided to put the infant up for adoption. He was at her side as she went through the labor and delivery, but the baby went home with another couple. That is when his whole world slowly began to fall apart.

He didn't know what was happening to him. He broke up with his girlfriend. He couldn't concentrate. He couldn't sleep well. He withdrew from his friends. He felt ashamed of himself. He thought his life was a failure at twenty-eight. He went to work every day and acted like his old lighthearted, carefree self. But after work he went home and hid alone in his apartment. He didn't want to see or talk to anybody. He hadn't learned how to tell his friends he felt awful. He had only learned how to act happy so they'd be charmed and enjoy being with him.

Andy was at the end of his rope, so he went to a family therapist. When he got there, he couldn't sift through his confusion to understand what was happening. All he could say was, "I'm confused." As he told me his story a year later, he said it was only in looking back that he could put the pieces into order and give them words.

His therapist had helped him see that a series of important losses early in his life had never been acknowledged. Now, giving up his own child to adoption and losing his girlfriend brought back all the grief he had put on the shelf long ago. The biggest loss of Andy's past came with his father's alcoholism. As a boy, he was repeatedly disappointed by his dad's unmet promises for fishing trips, a bicycle, or a birthday party. As alcohol increasingly took first place in his father's life, Andy gradually lost the close, admiring relationship he had. But he never really admitted that it made a difference to him.

After his therapist pointed this out, Andy said to me, "I started to acknowledge how many losses I had as a child. In doing so, I was introduced to 'Little

Andy.'" After learning this, he cried the tears he never shed as a child. The support he got from his therapist helped him explore his feelings. Andy said his tears caught him by surprise because, in a matter of a few weeks, he had gone from not knowing he really had any loss to "crying so hard I didn't know if I was crying or had the dry heaves. It was so intense I didn't know if I was going to pass out or ever stop. I had dropped off the edge of a cliff."

This powerful introduction of the man Andy to Little Andy was a striking development of a relationship in the spiritual realm. Little Andy was a mystery, an unexplained reality, a real force in the adult Andy's life that he hadn't known about. Little Andy was not a story or an idea. He came from the real experience of Andy's memory. Trusting his therapist, and then trusting his experience, introduced him to a spiritual realm.

It took courage and trust for Andy to let himself have such profound feelings. Because he took the risk to revisit his history and because he did not try to control the truth, he was introduced to a larger reality than he previously knew. After that introduction he learned, over time, to have a relationship with Little Andy. His therapist helped him use mental images of a good father with a son; by talking to his inner memories of Little Andy, Andy learned to give himself the love and caring he had missed.

Just as my relationship with our guest from Poland changed how I viewed my daily life, Andy's relationship with Little Andy, the childhood image of himself, changed his outlook on many things in his adult life. After becoming a kindly father to the little boy within, he developed a gentler attitude toward himself in other ways. He learned he didn't always have to present a happy, successful face to his friends. Today, Andy feels ready for a truly intimate relationship with a woman, and he hopes some day to have another chance at being a good father to his own child.

The Connection between Spirituality and Other Relationships

People have many kinds of relationships. You have relationships with your spouse, your friends, your children, your pets, and with inanimate things like your car, your tools, your favorite food, with money, or with a television show. The relationships you have with all these people and things in your life work together spiritually. One wise old saying suggests that the best way to know the true quality of a person's spiritual life or his religion is to look at his relationship with his neighbor. I notice that my relationships with myself, with nature, with God, with other men and women, and with our whole planet reflect back and forth. Our surroundings nurture and support us while we constantly influence our surroundings by our actions. The world is a little bit better place when we take care of ourselves. But, if we spit in our soup we have to eat spit. We cannot love others if we aren't loving toward ourselves. If I treat the child next door with disdain, it reflects back insidiously upon me.

In this era of individualism, it's important to remember that individualism can only work well when balanced with a sense of community. When I care for and work for the good of my neighbors, my community, and my fellow humans, then my efforts for individual advancement are just part of a larger spiritual harmony. But the worship of individualism and competitiveness, without honoring our relationship to other people and things, is simply personal advancement at others' expense.

False Faces

The roles people play and the facades they wear can block authentic intimate relationships. Andy's plunge into his past life was a return to honesty he never knew he was missing. His memories were real, but he had taken on roles and facades that covered them. He was charming and pleasing to his friends and co-workers, and they loved him. But they didn't really know him or what was happening in his life.

We all have false faces we wear, and we sometimes confuse them with our real selves. Some of them are the faces that go with our work: doctor, cab driver, welder. Others are roles we play like actors: the jock, the black sheep, the cool dude, the loser, the ladies man, the intellectual. The trouble is, we develop our faces and roles with our conscious, willful minds, thinking this will develop us as men. But such development is only surface polish. Our true self stays unlit and unexplored while we sharpen our external image. When our true self is covered up or lost behind our polished image, our spiritual life withers and dies. We may be successful in playing life as a game, but then the reality of life breaks through. Then, we need the strength and resourcefulness of our true self to deal with it.

When we encounter parts of our true self, it's usually a powerful experience as it was for Andy. Little Andy was no fashionable image that came from television. Little Andy came out of the truth as Andy remembered his experiences. His recall was painful, but it was honest, not something he constructed. So, as the man Andy got in touch with Little Andy, he became an authentic human being — a real man. When such an awakening of our authentic self occurs, it feels like we are filling out our spaces. It's like air is filling a balloon inside us to bring us to our natural shape. The image used in the Biblical creation story tells of God breathing life into man.

That image fits for the spiritual awakening of a modern man who gets in touch with his true experience.

How Does a Man Grow Spiritually?

No man grows spiritually simply because he decides to. The only control we have over our spiritual growth is the choice to either receive messages and learn from them, or block them. We can choose to take our personal, ordinary, daily experience and look for the messages it holds for us, or we can blandly disregard what happens in our lives, push aside its meaning, learn nothing from it.

For spiritual growth to happen, we have to let go of our attachment to rational, logical structure and risk the free-fall into nonrational experience. Facts are not always the same as truth. The leap of faith is a decision to rely sometimes on those things we cannot measure or prove objectively.

Let's say I step outside my front door in the morning to pick up the paper, and as I do, I trip on my cuff and fall. I am faced with a spiritual choice. I have scratched my hand, torn my pants and lost my composure. Perhaps I cuss about the loose cuff that tripped me, or I pull myself together and I berate myself for my awkwardness. With no spiritual orientation, I will feel that a random event, just bad luck, has struck, and now I alone must pull myself together so I can get ready for work. But if I choose an orientation that makes room for the mystery of life, I may look for a message in this event. It's not that God caused an accident to teach me a lesson. Bad luck strikes us all at times, and not because we deserve it or because God intended it for us. But, can we learn from it? Can we fall into a greater truth?

Perhaps my preoccupation with a troubling problem at work has been taking my attention away from other things in my life. My morning mishap may be a message to stop and take notice. I don't have to feel all alone in regaining my composure. As I go to the sink to wash the scratch and to my closet to find another pair of trousers, I can see myself as part of the world around me. What happens to me is what happens to all people. I can telephone a friend and tell him what has happened. As I feel the reality of our friendship while we talk, my spirit is restored.

Have you noticed when a television camera shows a close-up of a baseball pitcher after he has thrown a home run pitch, you can see the despair and agony flash across his face? That sight led writer David Huddle to wonder how a pitcher can return with confidence to pitch to the next batter. Somehow the pitcher has to take what just happened and use it for his growth. He must be ready to transform one painful experience into something that gives him the energy and strength to face the next batter. Huddle writes, "An instinctive response to painful experience is to avoid the behavior that produced the pain. To function at the level of excellence ... athletes must go against instinct, must absorb their failures and become stronger . . ."[2] Instead of withdrawing, the pitcher has to go right back into the next situation. He has to risk that he might do the same thing over again. If he holds back just a little, the next pitch will be just a little slower, just a little less than his best pitch. He must maintain a sense that he is in a process of growing and learning. He needs faith that putting himself in the same situation again will lead to a better performance.

Seeing Life as a Process

Taking the spiritual outlook, we see our whole life as a process. No matter how mixed up or difficult life gets, we are changing, going someplace. Sometimes, we feel like we're walking on a cleared path that's easy and beautiful. At other times, there is no path at all; we feel like we're trying to make it through thick wilderness where there is no sign that anyone is around to help us, and no sign of where we're headed. All we have to go on is faith that it will eventually lead us somewhere, that it will make sense later.

Your life is a process of becoming a better human being. You try to take whatever happens, big or small, and learn from it. You constantly get tired. Maybe you catch a cold and feel sick, or you eat too much, or you waste too much time watching television. The journey is not a state of constant balance and virtue. You naturally get off balance. Perfection isn't important. The key is you're always returning to the balance in which you are strong, healthy, well-rested, and unhurried so you can notice your experience and learn from it.

Theologian Matthew Fox says, "We're called to taste joy and to taste suffering. All mysticism [spirituality] is about experience. It can never be had vicariously. Adam's sin is that he didn't taste fully."[3] Fox means that the spiritual life is about tasting one's experience fully, being aware of and not holding back from life, not numbing it with chemicals, not covering it with diversions and not living through the stories and images we get from the shows and commercials on television. For some, simply noticing events and taking them in with all their senses is a way of listening to God. Others say it another way: that being attuned to your experience makes apparent a kind of wisdom that can't be expressed in straight line, logical reasoning. Whatever way you say it, having experiences and tasting them fully is essential to the spiritual process.

"Just be aware that you are on a spiritual search. . . ."

A friend of mine, just getting started in an Adult Children of Alcoholics group, was once having considerable difficulty with his spirituality. He said, "I don't believe in God. That stuff has never made any sense to me. But I want to recover in this program, so how can I go about becoming more spiritual?" I didn't feel very profound when he asked me this, but he has reminded me several times of my reply because he found it helpful. I told him, "Don't *work* at believing something. Just be aware that you are on a spiritual search. Notice what seems to speak honestly to you about the mystery or the unknown in your life. You can't decide to be spiritual, but you can decide to be open to spiritual questions." He used that thought as his beginning point. He went to his ACOA group where many people talked about a Higher Power in their lives. He talked to men and women who had a spiritual relationship with their Higher Power. Some he learned from, others he didn't. Gradually, his spiritual life opened up for him. He eventually followed a path back to the Jewish religion of his ancestors.

A Spiritual Relationship Grows with Regular, Faithful Contact

As with any relationship, an occasional chance meeting with our spiritual side may be pleasant, but that alone does not create a deep and lasting bond. Men opening their eyes to life and searching for spiritual growth often develop routines that help them practice spiritual growth. In recovery programs from addiction and codependency, people return weekly to their Twelve Step group. Some members go to more than one group each week. Routine attendance at a weekly meeting creates a pattern of returning faithfully to oneself, one's friends, and one's spiritual center.

Spiritual discipline changes a man. These aren't always sudden changes in one's personality, but usually a gradual evolution over months and years. I've known several men who were reluctant to talk to their wives or friends about the spiritual growth they had been accomplishing at AA or another Twelve Step group. They didn't expect anyone to notice anything different about them. Yet, they were surprised to be told by those who knew them well, "You have really changed recently. You have become much more relaxed and pleasant to be with."

Daily Inventory

The concept of discipline, as in training and practice, is an ancient method of spiritual development. One discipline of a Twelve Step program is the daily inventory of one's behavior. At the end of each day, a person reflects on his day to take stock. He may run through each event of the day, review his emotions, and hold himself accountable for his actions. He "promptly admits" his mistakes, misdeeds, or insensitivities to others. His goal is to stay current in his relationships with people as a way of growing spiritually. He cannot afford to allow unsaid apologies, unspoken thank-yous, or unacknowledged angers to pile up. If he does, they undermine the serenity upon which his recovery is based.

Prayer and Meditation

Another daily practice of the Twelve Steps is prayer and meditation. Individuals define differently what prayer and meditation are. Most people learn about it after they have begun to awaken spiritually. The important thing is to do it regularly. When a person returns again and again like a loyal friend to his time of prayer and meditation, it shapes him. It becomes a way of opening oneself to the impact of a Higher Power. Many people think of prayer as sitting or kneeling and speaking to God. That may be an effective way to pray. But as Henri Nouwen says in his book *Reaching Out*, prayer may be deep quiet in which one listens to what God has to say.

> Being useless and silent in the presence of our
> God belongs to the core of all prayer. In the begin-
> ning we often hear our own unruly inner noises
> more loudly than God's voice. This is at times very
> hard to tolerate. But slowly, very slowly, we dis-
> cover that the silent time makes us quiet and deep-
> ens our awareness of ourselves and God.[4]

If your idea of God is not a personal Being, you can still
pray. In that quiet listening, one's problems become more
clear, one's course of action may become decided. *The Meditative Mind,* by Daniel Goleman, is another helpful guide to
many traditional approaches to meditation.[5]

Creative Visualization

In working with very ill cancer patients in Texas, a physi-
cian-psychologist team, Carl and Stephanie Simonton, discovered the power of creative visualization for physical health.
They trained what were diagnosed as terminal cancer patients
to spend time every day quietly meditating and visualizing
the physical process of recovery. In doing so, these patients
significantly improved their chances of recovery. Of 159 patients, all were expected to die within a year, 19 percent of
them recovered completely. Those who didn't recover and
eventually died of their illness lived twice as long as their
predicted survival time. The Simontons created mental exercises that are now used all over the country to improve
chances of recovery for cancer patients. In simple terms, the
patient begins with a few minutes of deep relaxation. After
becoming fully relaxed and putting aside all distractions, he or
she imagines cancer cells being eaten and destroyed by
healthy cells.

Using similar methods, surgeon Bernie Siegel works with
cancer patients to use their spiritual side to enhance their

overall health. He started an organization of people recovering from cancer called Exceptional Cancer Patients to help them mobilize all of their resources for health. He described his work in a book called *Love, Medicine, and Miracles*.[6]

Hypnosis with mental imagery has become a well-docmented and common practice for psychotherapists treating specific phobias such as fear of flying, fear of crossing bridges, or anxiety when taking a test. In a trance created by deep relaxation, a person is taught to visualize comforting and safe images to get a new outlook on the feared experience. Returning daily to the same comforting and safe image can effectively reduce or totally free a person from a phobia.

Spiritual people of Far Eastern, Western, and tribal traditions have used similar techniques throughout history. Using powers of imagination seems a uniquely human thing to do — and seems to enhance our humanness. Mental imagery opens up, right before our eyes, new possibilities that we didn't know existed. It restores our physical health, provides a new vision for our daily life, and leads us in a spiritual direction. Like the baseball pitcher who takes failure and transforms it into positive, creative energy, we can create images for strength and health when we are under stress or having other problems. Many audio tapes are now available that teach the use of relaxation and self-hypnosis for mental imagery. Some focus on specific goals like quitting smoking, and others for broader goals such as general stress reduction.

Music and Nature

Listening to music or playing and singing are the most spiritual experiences in the lives of many people. Others regularly turn to nature as the doorway. A walk through the woods, a day in a fishing boat, or an hour in the garden puts them into contact with something larger than themselves.

Friendships

The development and maintenance of friendships can be a path to the spiritual life for recovering men. Being a friend and having one creates a different attitude toward life than the "master of my own fate" outlook. A caring and honest friendship grows as two people begin to truly get to know each other. It builds on their experience together in many different situations, and it takes time.

Sooner or later, the day comes when you planned a round of golf with your friend, but something has happened that upset you. Maybe your boss has given you a bad work evaluation; maybe you and your wife have had a big fight; maybe you're worried about the nagging pain in your stomach. Now you're faced with the choice between telling your friend what's really happening or simply going to play golf and acting like it's just another normal day for you.

An authentic friendship is one where you talk about the real stuff. At times, you will have some conflict as the relationship moves to the level where it truly matters to you. But as it becomes more real, it nourishes your spirit. (More about friendships will be discussed in Chapter Six.)

Reading

Reading for pleasure, whether it be a detective story, a travel magazine, or a good novel may be an enhancement to a man's spiritual life. Even if it isn't specifically spiritual reading, just relaxing and taking a break for pleasure opens a person to spiritual growth. More specifically, reading and study of scriptures and spiritual writings put you in touch with the yearnings and answers that other seekers like yourself have recorded over the centuries. I like to turn to the Book of Psalms to read about David's strivings. I find honest, kindred spirits there. Sometimes David was at his wit's end with problems, and at other times he was elated about simply being alive. We can share his journey, thousands of years later, on a day when we're at our wit's end, or when we're elated about being alive, by reading his words.

Journal Writing

Sitting with a pencil and paper to write is another method of spiritual growth. Do it every day if you can, or every few days. I have notes I've written, simply for my own benefit, that go back fifteen years. Sometimes I wrote every day for weeks. Other years, I wrote only three or four times. I use an inexpensive notebook and begin each entry by putting the date at the top of the page and my location at the moment of writing. I have many entries headed with a date and "sitting at the kitchen table." Others were written at memorable times like sitting in a park while on vacation, or in my room while on retreat. After the heading, I write whatever comes to mind. It helps me to start with a specific topic, but then I just let my mind go wherever it will. I try not to take conscious control or make myself stay on any one subject. If I run out of things to write, I keep writing by saying, "Now I've run out of things to say." A writing teacher I took a class from, Natalie Goldberg, has written a book on this subject called *Writing Down the Bones*.[7] In it are excellent ideas on how to get more fully acquainted with your inner truths, or the deeper anxieties you wouldn't otherwise know you were carrying around. Writing is good at revealing these things.

Living through the Flat Times

In following a spiritual path, our days are not always exciting. Much of our time seems ordinary. Crisis and struggle are hard and painful, but times of emotional and spiritual flatness are often more difficult to handle. I want every one of my days to have great significance. But most feel like just another day. Even these ordinary days are part of the spiritual life. Sometimes I feel alienated. Life is not always wonderful and positive. That is when the patterns of spiritual practice carry me along like the momentum of a rolling stone. I don't have to decide every day if I feel like praying or if I feel in contact with nature in order to continue my spiritual activities. Sometimes, I just do them out of faithfulness to routine, and by the time I've completed my routine I feel reunited with my spiritual source. Other times, I just feel like I've been true to myself.

A Spiritual Life Integrates Us

In the end, a relationship with forces greater than himself pulls a man together into wholeness. He starts with a sense of painful brokenness, incompleteness, and imperfection. He grows toward a feeling of integrity and wholeness. The word *whole* in the English language grew from the same root word as *health* and *holy*. In Old English *hal* meant "healthy," "sound," and "happy." That is what spiritual health and wholeness is. The integrity, the wholeness that grows as a gift of the spiritual life, is a gathering together of a man's fragmented parts so that they can work together to create strength. Spirituality makes a man more loving, more productive, more self-accepting, more playful, and more in contact with the whole, rich range of his emotional life.

CHAPTER 4

Shame: Feeling Alone in the Pit of Unworthiness

> *Being Human is difficult.*
> *Becoming human is a life-long process.*
> *To be truly human is a gift.*
> *-- Abraham Heschel*

He walked into my office and gave me the standard greeting, "Hi, Merle, how are you?" But the tone of his voice was more tense than usual. His eyes looked like black marbles set in granite. As we sat down to begin his weekly therapy session, he first gasped for air, then let out a deep sigh, and said, "I need to tell you something I've never told anyone before in my life."

The moment for him had arrived to take the risk. Still, he couldn't quite get it out. He stood on the brink of a new reality in his life. Up to that moment, he had total control over a secret that he had kept totally within himself. No one else in the world knew. Now, he was about to break and let one other person know. This shift from having no one else know to letting someone else know was a huge personal change.

I understood when he hesitated a moment there on the brink. He hemmed and hawed as if standing atop a high diving board. He said, "Maybe you won't think it's all that big a deal. I suppose you hear this kind of thing all the time."

My imagination was running miles ahead. I thought of a dozen terrible secrets a man might be carrying around. Did he kill somebody as a teenager? Has he been embezzling money from his company? Is he cheating on his wife?

Finally he blurted it out. "I'm hooked on pornography. I've been buying magazines with erotic pictures of women for years. I cut out my favorite pictures and save them in locked files at home. When I'm alone I go through them, I arrange and sort them as if they were my private harem. I can lose hour after hour in fantasies with those pictures. I often masturbate with them. I've tried to throw them all out, but I can't. It feels like I'm throwing away my best friends. I've always told myself that this doesn't hurt anybody, but I'm not so sure anymore. I don't think my wife knows anything about this, but it makes me feel like a total scum bag after I waste half a day in a secret fantasy. It makes me depressed. My wife knows I get depressed, but she doesn't know why. I tell her I don't know why either, but that's a lie. I've promised myself a thousand times I'll never buy another magazine, but suddenly on my lunch break, there I am again, in a sleazy bookstore buying another one."

Defining Shame and Guilt

The man with his secret was awash in shame. *Guilt* and *shame* are often used as words with the same meaning. But I've learned in my psychotherapy practice and my personal life that big doors open for people in their growth when they understand the important difference between the two words.

Shame is feeling hopelessly awful about yourself as a person. A shameful man may say these sorts of things to himself: *I am less than other people. As a person, as a man, at my core, I'm not good enough, or I'm not smart enough, or I'm bad, or inadequate, or ugly. If other people really knew me, they wouldn't like me. I can make no honest bridge to others. I must find ways to relate that don't rely on honesty. I can only have friends if I put on a good face or charm them and hide the deeper unfinished, chaotic parts of myself.*

Guilt, on the other hand, is a painful feeling about my actions, not my worth as a person. It's knowing I'm just like everyone else in my imperfection and incompleteness. It's regretting having made a mistake or having done something that violated my values. It's knowing that my behavior has consequences, and that I feel badly about them when they hurt others or myself.

For example, I feel guilty about thoughtlessly forgetting to meet a friend for lunch after setting the appointment with him. I know he arranged his schedule to be there as we agreed, and then he sat alone waiting for me and I never showed up. That doesn't mean I'm a bad person; it means I made a mistake. I feel guilty when, opening a door, I bump a little child on the opposite side and knock her down. It hurts me to know my actions hurt a child, even if it was unintentional. Guilt is being in tune with my impact on others. No one can be an active, caring person without feeling guilt at times. It's a healthy, human feeling.

Shame is about myself as a person. Guilt is about my behavior. With guilt, I keep my self-respect. Out of the pain of guilt, I try to find a way to make repairs — to make things right again. But no repair is possible from the perspective of shame. Shame destroys my self-respect and dignity. There is no fixing it up, no repair, no way back. It leads to no personal growth. The only responses to shame is to cover up, hide, or run away. Sometimes people cover their shame by putting on a very smooth, perfect exterior, and by keeping secrets. Sometimes they run away by simply disappearing from friendships.

Shame Is More Than Low Self-Esteem

Early in my career as a family therapist, I spent nine months with a great teacher, Virginia Satir, in a small, intensive family therapy training program in Palo Alto, California. My work with her changed my life both personally and professionally. Her central theme for our group was this: *self-esteem is the main issue in emotional well-being*. We examined self-esteem as it develops in small children, and we worked to improve impaired self-esteem in children with problems. We worked with couples and saw how their relationships were troubled because of low self-esteem. We studied the self-esteem factors in good and bad communication. Virginia's definition of high self-esteem went like this: *high self-esteem is when my image of myself matches my image of how I should be.*

Years after my intensive training with her, I learned more about alcoholism. It is a disease often carried within the family from one generation to the next. In a similar way, the abused child of one generation may be the abusive parent in the next. Observing these generational patterns with my own eyes again and again had a great impact on me. We can work in therapy on self-esteem; people can have powerful successes in their careers and esteem-building experiences with friends, but still they return again and again like migrating swallows, even against their conscious will, to the same self-destructive patterns of prior generations. The great theoretical question in the field of family therapy has moved from, "How can we promote change?" to "Why do things stay so much the same?"

What Virginia Satir taught about self-esteem was my beginning point, my base to build on as I grew professionally. At first, I had thought of self-esteem almost as if we each had a thermometer by which we could gauge higher or lower self-esteem. I didn't see that its opposite, self-hate or shame, has its own momentum apart from self-esteem. I don't recall how or when the concept of shame as a psychological term came into my field of view. I know that other therapist colleagues were interested in it, too, and we learned from each other.

My friend and colleague, Dr. Marilyn J. Mason, and I worked as co-therapists with several families, and several ideas about shame as a hidden dynamic in family relations developed out of our work. Ultimately, we wrote a book together called *Facing Shame: Families in Recovery.*[1]

One important idea I learned shows how the dynamics of self-hate work — that shame begets more shame. It is not just a low reading on the thermometer of self-esteem. Shame is something like cancer — it grows on its own momentum. Positive self-esteem experiences don't fully overcome the negative corrosion of shame unless a person faces it directly.

The man who compulsively shamed himself by immersion in pornography ritually degraded himself. He revitalized his shame feelings over and over again with his actions, just as the father does who reenacts the abuse his father wrought on him when he abuses his child. No amount of friends, no amount of job success or marital happiness, or other positive experiences, as helpful and encouraging as they are, will block the cancer of self-defeating behavior in these men until they confront their shame directly. To focus on the moral questions of pornography doesn't help him because it isn't a guilt problem; it's a shame problem. Finding acceptable images for him to view or helping him feel better about what he is doing don't touch the heart of his problem. Regardless of the behavior, men burdened by shame first need to stop the behavior that actively revitalizes their shame, and then they need to face their underlying shame issues.

What Are Men Ashamed Of?

The experience of shame, whether male or female, comes out of a feeling that our humanness is diminished, that we don't fully qualify as members of the human community, that we aren't good enough to be accepted and loved as we are.

Shame transcends gender. The waste and hurt is as bad for either sex. Yet, it seems different things trigger shame responses in men than in women.

Weakness

For example, problems that show weakness might bring up shame in men. Most men automatically think they ought to deal with their problems alone and be cool and unfeeling about them. A job problem, a health problem, or a family problem can bring feelings of weakness. Naturally, these problems come along for everyone as part of life. So men cannot avoid shame unless they find other ways of coping besides expecting to be strong and stoically "toughing it out."

In contrast, women in our culture are far more accepting of weakness. Of course, it feels good to be strong, but vulnerability doesn't raise doubts about a woman's femininity. When a problem comes along, they are more comfortable telling friends what is going on, and maybe crying together about it. Women don't have the self-esteem barrier to cross before accepting help. This flexibility gives them stronger coping methods for dealing with the normal life set-backs and crises that can't be avoided.

Body Image

Both men and women are highly subject to shame about body issues. Anyone with a scar, a birthmark, even a bruise knows the power of body image to trigger shame. Physical disabilities can pose profound challenges to a person's self-respect, not because there is anything shameful about them, but because it challenges a person to answer, "My dignity has nothing to do with my physical image or strength."

Sexual Performance

It seems to me that men are especially subject to shame about sex and sexual performance. If a man's sexual performance isn't satisfactory to his mate, he is likely to feel shameful and want to hide the fact. We live in a culture that tells men to be the sexual sophisticates. That is a hurtful myth because it doesn't match the reality at least half of the time. When a man doesn't fulfill the sophisticate image, he may feel he is less of a man. Any problem with sex in a relationship may feel like *his* responsibility and a sign of failure.

Providing for Family

The good provider image is a big one for men. When this image is not fulfilled, either because of limited opportunity to work, lack of skills, or job loss due to economic changes, a man's shame can be triggered. When a man has job problems, he can be under just as much stress from the shame as from the financial pressure. He thinks he should be in control. If a man isn't meeting his father's goals for him in a career or isn't achieving as much out in the world as his father did, he may feel like a failure.

Shame and Our Fathers

To move psychologically out of childhood into adulthood, a man must transpose his father's standards and goals for him into a new version that fits him. If he never got complete acceptance and approval from his dad, he may stay focused on a deep feeling that something is wrong with him. If he never got beyond anger and rebellion against what his dad stood for, his emancipation remains incomplete, and he may carry shame until he can let go of that anger. Facing shame and healing from it means respecting ourselves. For many of us, that means coming to terms with our fathers and making peace with them.

Seeing our fathers as separate people on their own life journey, just as we are on our life journey, and accepting our fathers allows us to accept ourselves. When we can deal with our fathers in the flesh, it helps us get beyond those shame and emancipation hurdles. Childhood images of our fathers may have been bigger than life, seeing them as either a hero or a devil. As adults, our images don't mature without person-to-person experience in learning to know the real man. He has thoughts and feelings, doubts and imperfect choices. Knowing him within the same human dimensions that we live our own lives and still respecting him creates a base for our own self-respect. Other men help, too, and they can serve as a stand-in for our father if he isn't available.

Facing Hardships

Many men believe the most admirable trait is to endure hardship without flinching. But this trait makes them so rigid it can create a blindness to the reality of their own feelings. Thus, they become less adaptable to change. I remember one instance when that belief was reinforced in my life. It made me very angry. It was at my grandmother's funeral. My father's mother died at the age of ninety-one; my father was sixty-eight years old. After the funeral service a few tears rolled down his cheeks. The pastor noticed them and I suspect he intended to bolster Dad by challenging him to recapture his stoic facade. His response to Dad's tears were, "Leif, I always thought you were stronger than that!" I was furious at the pastor because my father had the right to feel grief at his mother's death. I was also proud of my father for his integrity and honesty in feeling his grief and feeling his attachment to his mother.

Having feelings, and releasing our control to face them as they are, takes courage and is more dignified than squelching them. Hiding and stuffing our feelings may give the external appearance of control and strength, but experiencing them makes us more genuinely strong and flexible for coping with life and moving on.

The "Wounded Father" Image

The writer Samuel Osherson, in his book *Finding Our Fathers*, describes an image some men have of their fathers called the "wounded father." Men who grew up with a "wounded" father often feel sorry for their dads and carry a sense of shame through adult life, never knowing it really originated with their dads, not themselves. One man I met struggles with that kind of self-hate. It began with his excruciating embarrassment for his father: as a boy, his father became a community spectacle when he was fired from his job as school superintendent for accepting a bribe.

Another man always felt his father was no match in a fight with his mother. He pitied his father for his inadequacies and tried to protect him. But since he was protective, he couldn't ever test his own strength against his dad. He never went through an adolescent rebellion during which he could say a loud "No!" to his father. He was always afraid his own power might be too hurtful, so he never learned to trust and accept his power. And he could never respect himself any more than he respected his father.

The "Male Ego"

The *male ego* is a term I hear women use. Sometimes its called the *fragile male ego*. What I think they are talking about is a man's susceptibility to shame. I think women see something about us that we don't see ourselves. We can learn from them if we listen.

Women tell us that many of them have taken on the job of propping men up, helping maintain a man's image of strength and power, being careful not to challenge men so strongly that their weak spots get exposed. This seems to be women's awareness of men's shame. They tell us they've learned that if certain buttons get pushed, a man gets defensive, angry, shameful, or he goes away. Women are naturally quite ambivalent about the whole thing. On one hand, they try to treat men gently because they don't want to be hurtful or abandoned; on the other hand, they're angry about maintaining this charade instead of having a more intimate relationship. Sometimes women laugh about this thing they see in men because it looks so silly from the outside.

As a man grows in recovery, he learns that his buttons, his weak spots, belong to himself. How he feels is not the fault of someone who pushed his buttons. He takes on his own feelings and deals with the discomfort without shame. He doesn't expect his wife or lover to play the role of Weak Violet or the Dumb Blond to make him look stronger and smarter.

Wading through the Stream of Shame

To understand the sources of shame, think of all of your daily activities as a giant landscape. You have your work, your friends and family relationships, meals, money management, home and car maintenance. Now, imagine an expanse that you wander through containing hills and buildings, trees, roads, and rivers. Each feature in this landscape represents a part of your life. Some features are very prominent because they represent activities you spend a great deal of time with, while others are far back in a corner you see only occasionally.

Imagine that from time to time as you wander your landscape of daily activity, you suddenly plunge into the stream of shame. Sometimes you see it coming. Sometimes it happens without warning; you just end up in the water with all your clothes on. No matter how you got there, it always feels cold and dirty and smells bad.

Most people have no awareness that they are actually landing in the same stream every time. The fact that you stumble on a shame event today when your boss asks you a question is directly connected to the fact that you learned the shame response in your past. It is a stream that has a source or several sources. The original source of your stream of shame may not be in view anymore, but it exists. If you become more acquainted with your stream, you won't have to be such a victim of it or go swimming in it quite as often.

Sources of Shame

As Marilyn Mason and I worked together, she named the three main sources of shame that we found:

- the traumatic origin,
- the inherited generational origin, and
- maintained shame.

Traumatic Origin of Shame

The traumatic origin for shame is the specific experience in your life of being treated badly and having your dignity or innocence stolen from you. This includes all the ways that you may have been put down, abused, made a scapegoat, ridiculed, blamed, used, or neglected. These experiences leave scars. People often don't remember the events, but these events taught them how to feel unworthy. Or, they do remember them, but they discount the events because they insist they're not affected by them.

Bad treatment of boys often gets dismissed as toughening up for manhood. The scars that form the lifelong stream of shame for adult men are too often dismissed and ignored. Trying to create an image of toughness and covering memories of the abuse and the shame it instilled, is one of the ways development of genuine masculine strength gets stifled.

If we are treated inhumanly, we feel degraded and ashamed. Something has been stolen from us — our dignity. Such abuse can be more devastating for children than for adults because children don't understand what is happening. When a child is brutalized or is quietly treated badly, he may not even know that it is wrong or unfair. Still, his dignity is stolen and shame quickly becomes part of his identity.

We can see how this happens most clearly in a victim of an ordeal like a serious car accident, a fire, a mugging, or a hostage crisis. The fallout from that trauma goes on for a long time after the event is over. The victim can become extremely nervous, sleepless, and tortured with self-doubt and inadequacy long after the event, even though the victim was in no way to blame. Ongoing abuse has a similar impact but may not be as easy to identify as one big terrible event.

Inherited Generational Origin of Shame

Inherited generational origins of shame first became known to me in my work with adults who could find no traumatic incidents in their own history. Yet they had all the vulnerability to shame that victims of traumatic shaming have. When we looked, we found shaming events in prior generations, like the father of a client who was abandoned by his parents at the age of ten. It was a family secret that felt too awful for the father to tell his son about until the son came asking questions. The stream of shame flowed, not just in the lifetime of my client, but from a source in a previous generation unknown to him, into his own present experience.

The mother of one deeply shameful client was the childhood victim of incest. Other clients came from generations of brutal, abusive racism and anti-Semitism. Basic human dignity was stolen from their parents, grandparents, and great-grandparents, and the shame response, once seeded in the family's emotional climate, was active in a man's present life. In the inherited shame process, families adopt rules of behavior that are meant to defend them against shame. But in reality, the rules of behavior hide the shame and allow it to be passed unwittingly from generation to generation.

Eight Rules of the Shame-Bound Family

Rule number one: *Be in control at all times.*[2]

This rule leads people in a family to control themselves and to keep everyone predictable. It squelches spontaneity because people are afraid if they are spontaneous they'll get abused and look bad to other family members. Many family members become extremely manipulative as they try to follow this rule. Some gain control by being domineering, others by being ill, and still others by being sweet and pleasing.

Rule number two: *Always be right, do the right thing.*

We call this "the perfection rule" because it doesn't allow room for the natural human process of making mistakes and learning from experience. The humanness of imperfection is squelched by this rule. Everyone is imperfect so people feel a little less honest with themselves as they try to follow it. Either they get so good at it that they cover their shame with self-righteousness, or they have a feeling of failure because only the impossible (perfection) is acceptable.

Rule number three: *If something doesn't happen as planned, blame someone, yourself or another person.*[3]

With this rule, surprise or puzzlement is almost always cause for attaching blame. "If you were different, I could be happy." "Why do you always have your foot in my way?" "If I hadn't talked about the weather, we would have had a sunny day." "It's your fault that I put my fist through the wall because you made me angry." These are examples of things that might be said in a family that lives by this rule.

Rule number four: *Deny feelings, especially the negative or vulnerable ones like anxiety, fear, loneliness, grief, rejection, or need.*

I've sat with families who follow this rule, and, as I got acquainted with them, I began to feel a deep sense of underlying loneliness or sadness in their stories. I could even see those feelings show on their faces. But when I told them about it they were totally unaware of the feelings themselves. They said, "Oh no, you don't understand. We don't feel that way at all," and they were not consciously lying. They actually didn't know what they felt. So these families are never able to share feelings because they can't admit them.

Rule number five: *Don't expect reliability or constancy in relationships.*

We found wide variations in the quality of contact between people in these families, with little consistency from one encounter to the next. One time a couple may be like a pair of lovebirds, and the next day, for no apparent reason, one will withdraw, creating great emotional distance. Or they may have an intense crisis over a conflict and, without ever resolving anything, they somehow put the problem aside and carry on as if nothing had ever happened. These families need an outside person, such as a therapist, to ask the question: "How did you get from point A to point B?" They often answer something like, "I don't know. It didn't seem important." In fact, they probably feel the abrupt switches and psychological disappearances are normal. It is therapeutic for them to look at transitions and question the process of mood swings within their family system.

Rule number six: *Don't bring transactions or disagreements to completion or resolution.*

With this rule, people living with shame, covering secrets, or hiding from themselves are fearful of reaching conclusions. Some are deeply afraid of conflict, so they flee from it. They don't realize that if you don't engage in some conflict, you can never resolve anything. Then differences just get stored up and accumulate in an underlying tension between otherwise loving people. Some may be frightened of being held accountable or blamed for the decisions they make. Others may be simply continuing what they learned to do as children with no greater reason for doing it than it's the only way they know.

Rule number seven: *Don't talk openly and directly about shameful, abusive, or compulsive behavior in our family.*

I first became acquainted with this pattern in families with alcoholism and other drug addiction. It's often true that the neighbors know before family members that someone's drug use is out of control. Family members feel deeply blocked from talking about it; they can't put their heads together to figure out what is going on. Adults who were sexually abused as children may have specific memories of the abusive experiences and yet wonder if they were abused or not. Since it was never acknowledged, they really don't know how to understand it.

Rule number eight: *When disrespectful, shameful, abusive or compulsive behavior occurs, disqualify it, deny it, or disguise it.*

No one following this rule would say, "Grandpa Ben is alcoholic." They might say, "He has a little too much to drink once in a while." In another family, the abused child is blamed for provoking the parent's rage, rather than the parent admitting directly that he or she lost control in punishing the child. Abuse gets laughed at as if it were one of the family jokes. Overeating may be explained as a healthy appetite.

These eight rules describe a pattern of relationships, and yet every family is different and many of these rules overlap. If you see yourself and your family communication in any of these rules, you have something to put your finger on. They are ways that shame gets perpetuated in your life. It gets passed on to your children in the same ways. No one can change their family rules simply by saying, "Now I see it and I won't do that anymore." It's never that easy. Yet, knowing it, naming it, and having a label for it makes it different already. It gives you a handle you can grasp; then it's something you can work on. You no longer have to be in the dark or mystified by falling into the stream of shame. You no longer need to believe you alone deserve to be ashamed, because now you've got ways to understand its true source. Over time, with attention to the pattern, and with help, you will change.

Maintained Shame

The source of shame called maintained shame was exemplified at the opening of this chapter by the man addicted to pornography. It refers to any action or behavior a person engages in, often for pleasure, that has the side effect of abusing his self. Sometimes the loss of control is degrading; sometimes the invasion of boundaries is disrespectful; sometimes the violation of one's fundamental values is so great that the shame response is inevitable. In maintained shame, the repetition of actions that degrade one's self is the crucial factor. Anyone with an addictive or compulsive behavior is probably maintaining his shame and may not even know it.

The Shame-Rage Connection

Gershen Kaufman, the author of *Shame: The Power of Caring,* identified the way in which intense anger or rage can serve as a cover for shame.[4] He wrote that a person who flies into rage may feel suddenly exposed or in danger of looking like a fool. I think it's a common connection for men who have problems with anger attacks. They may never know that their underlying shame or self-hate was tapped. The only thing that shows on the outside is a sudden, uncontrollable, and even abusive rage.

An Example of Shame Covered by Rage

I have a friend who has a long-standing relationship with some fishing buddies. This group has been together for about fifteen years, and they go on fishing trips to Canada twice a year. Between trips they get together in twos and threes for lunch when they can and for an occasional evening out with their wives. These men know each other very well.

One spring, one of the men, Jed, began to act very moody and distant. The guys talked about him because they couldn't understand what was going on. The gossip in the community was spreading that Jed was doing a lot of gambling and was in deep financial trouble. But he never told his friends about it. So they decided the best way to be good friends was to talk directly to him. They decided to do that the following Wednesday when they were to meet and plan for the upcoming fishing opener.

His closest friend in the group, Bill, began by saying he had heard some things from his neighbor and wanted to hear straight from Jed what was going on. Jed instantly flew into anger. His face turned red with rage as he yelled that Bill was an S.O.B. and accused him of spreading malicious rumors. Everyone sat in silent shock at the intensity of Jed's attack. When he quit yelling, Jed stormed out of the house, didn't go on the fishing trip, and refused to talk to anyone in the group for weeks afterward.

The friends all felt abused by his rage and misunderstood. They vaguely wondered if they had done it wrong. Yet, they were sure that Jed's anger was abusive and out of bounds. This was a clear example of underlying shame that was covered by rage. Sadly, Jed's shame got perpetuated by his outburst and by his cutting off of the friendships, so no repair or resolution could be made.

The Shame/Self-Righteousness Connection

As we studied family systems that have a problem with shame, we usually found one or more members of the family who felt pious, better than others, unrealistically self-satisfied, or grandiose. These individuals seemed to be unaware of their own feelings of shame, but they lived in a family system where others felt very shameful. These self-righteous people are often critical; they say they hold high standards, and in many ways are quite successful in controlling their behavior. But they are unhappy and may not have close relationships with anyone. They are not aware of their motivations and they don't realize how much their self-righteousness comes from a symbiotic relationship with the less-successful, less-powerful family members.

For example, a husband may be always critical of his wife. She accepts it and feels inadequate until one day he suddenly dies of a heart attack. Following her grief, she comes into her own. She no longer is loaning him her strength and self-respect by being one down to make him feel strong. She becomes a much more effective person. No one ever knew he was depending on her to feel good about himself. His self-righteousness was really covering his underlying feelings of shame. He had the same stolen dignity and pain that other shameful people have, but it was hidden by a life pattern of control and arrogant self-righteousness. Neither he nor she could grow out of their shame until that symbiotic pattern was broken, either by greater honesty or by death.

Recovery from Shame

Of all my work with men and women in therapy, to walk the path with a client out of shame into self-respect is the most rewarding experience. That walk is as awesome as any wilderness experience I have ever had with towering mountain walls and raging waterfalls, and as tender as a healing stream in warm sunshine. A man's confrontation with his personal, private human core is profound. Facing our shame teaches us what true humanity is. We all have shame to face within ourselves because we all have been treated badly in one way or another and felt diminished. We all have violated ourselves in some way. We all are bombarded daily by depersonalizing messages. The rampant racism, sexism, materialism, drug orientation, and militarism around us diminishes our value as individuals. These evil forces cause human beings to be treated like objects and undermines our self-respect. So, if you feel you have work to do, you are not alone. We all have a lifelong task of becoming truly human rather than settling for indignity and shame.

Maxwell Maltz is quoted as saying, "You must fight off a 'bad luck' way of thinking as if you were dealing with an invasion of hostile forces — for that is precisely what you are dealing with." After you become aware of your shame feelings, the next thing to do for your recovery is to make a solemn vow. Promise that you will no longer give your energy to hostility against yourself, to self-derogatory or self-hating purposes. Make a conscious decision to be on your own side, because there are enough harmful forces and events coming from outside yourself that would abuse you, put you down, or hurt you. Naturally, making the vow doesn't mean you can suddenly, willfully change. But it sets a standard for you to imperfectly adhere to, and keep returning to.

Many men are naive and they say, "I have no enemies!" These men are certain to get hurt. You need to know you have enemies; identify who and what they are, and be certain not to join their side. Your enemies include the depersonalizing forces just mentioned and those family rules that instill and perpetuate your shame. They also include inner attitudes of self-hate and hopelessness, and any people who diminish your recovery, strength, and health. You join your enemies when you mope around, mentally criticizing your basic nature. Your solemn promise means that you no longer berate yourself for your mistakes or indulge in the habit of calling yourself shameful or gutter names when you feel low. Leave that activity to your enemies. You can make mistakes. You can feel sad or ashamed. That's human. But, you begin the road out of shame by using your conscious mind and your will to befriend yourself. You consciously say the things to yourself that you would say to a dear, respected friend. "God loves you. You are a child of the universe. You deserve a place here like everyone else. You have a right to make mistakes." Another phrase my mother often used was, "It takes all kinds of people to make a world." Claim it as your right to be one kind of a person in a varied world!

Barriers to Recovery from Shame

Break down the alienation and invisible barriers between you and other people. You can do this in concrete and practical ways. For instance, have no secrets that aren't shared with someone. Everyone needs at least two or three people who know them very well. Certainly, some things you have to say won't make you look good, but with a trusted friend you don't always have to look good. Only a statue can be perfect, and even then it casts a shadow. Say to yourself, *I don't want to be a cold, lifeless statue. I want to be alive, a thriving human being with passion and feeling.* So let down your control over what your friends know. Let a few people know you as you are. As you let another person know you, you also get to know yourself. Expect your friends to accept you as you are.

Not Telling the Whole Story

It is also possible to keep up a barrier by telling only parts of your story to a person and telling other parts to someone else. Then you can say that you have told everything to someone. Still, no one person has all the pieces. No one really knows you totally, and you continue to feel vaguely mistrustful and alone, and your shame is preserved.

How Therapy Can Help

Sometimes taking down all barriers begins with help from a therapist. It is a safe place to let go of all private memories, thoughts, and feelings and to get a therapist's reactions. But therapy alone isn't enough. You must take that honesty outside the setting of the therapist's office and risk letting a trusted few know you with nothing held back. This kind of relationship builds over time; it doesn't suddenly happen in one conversation. When it does happen, you can have the elation and release of knowing you are accepted by others who really know you.

Catching Fire

Leaving Relationships

Some of the shame a man feels may get perpetuated by simply disappearing from his relationships. Perhaps he has a friendship he cares about; then one day tension develops between him and his friend. Maybe he did something he feels badly about, or his friend did something he's mad about. The shameful response is to simply drop the relationship. No explanation, he just drops out of contact. Within families, people who grew up together — brothers, sisters, parents — may stop talking for years. The noted family therapist, Murray Bowen, studied these cut offs within families, and he found that they prevent people from maturing and becoming strong individuals.

Disappearing from relationships is like taking a bunch of freshly picked string beans, blanching them, and sticking them in the freezer. All growth and change stops abruptly. Six months later you take them out of the freezer, and they're almost like the day you picked them. That's what we want with string beans but not with our lives. When a twenty-year-old man is thinking like a twenty-year-old, he is emotionally healthy and alive. But, when a thirty-year-old still thinks like a twenty-year-old, he has missed ten years of personal development and growth. Cutting off relationships, disappearing from them, refusing to talk or even to say good-bye, freezes a man's shame. It saves a man from having to deal with it head-on, but it also preserves it within him until it is dealt with honestly.

If you have old friends that once meant a lot to you and you abruptly dropped the relationship, or if you have parents, brothers, or sisters you've stopped all meaningful contact with, rid yourself of shame by contacting them. If this is going to work, you must do it with empathy for the other person. In some situations more harm is done by making contact, and silence is the most considerate choice. But in most cases,

82

reestablishing contact, with a willingness to make apologies when necessary, is like a long-awaited homecoming. That's how shame can flow normally out of your life rather than storing it up in your mind.

Humility and Shame Are Two Different Traits

I used to think humility was the paradoxical virtue of being good because you thought you were bad. I thought it was almost the same as shame. But I've had several good talks about it with my male friends. It has become clear that humility is not the same as shame at all. In fact, shame and humility do not coexist in the same person. Humility is when a man with self-respect knows he has a place and a relationship with other people, with the world, with the cosmos, with the flow of time through the centuries. Humility is when a man doesn't presume to inflate, diminish, or in any way manipulate the image of where he fits in. Humility is to accept a leadership role and success for what it is when it comes, and to accept defeat with the same attitude.

From this truly humble perspective, we know we are more similar than different from others. We are the tiniest speck of dust in the infinite universe, with a lifetime as brief as a flash compared to the flow of billions of years of creation. Yet, the most admirable story is one where a person overcomes the obstacles to his dignity to make progress in the face of great difficulty, or when someone performs heroic acts of looking out for another person. Life is a risk for anyone who loves and cares about others and who tries to grow. If you say, "But it's so hard!" my reply is, "Yes, of course it is hard. But there is no alternative except stagnation or death. So why not get into the act and enjoy it?"

EXERCISES FOR FACING YOUR SHAME

- What memories do you have of feeling that your dignity as a person was ridiculed or stripped away? How did you recover from that? Or are you still living with that indignity as if it has power over you? You can begin the healing of these memories by talking to someone about them.

- Do you have old friends or family members who once were important to you, but you have not contacted? Consider what it would take for you to bridge that gap. Would it be healing to write a letter and make amends? Would a telephone call be worth a risk to repair your shame? If you do this, it's best to talk to someone else about it beforehand to get his or her advice about it.

- Can you name any ways that you are habitually maintaining your shame? Were there some ways in your past that are not present today?

- If you give the entire job of opposing your enemies to your enemies, you are free to put your whole self into being healthy, successful, and self-accepting. Write three sentences of support that an honest friend might say to you.

CHAPTER 5

Getting to Know Your Family System

The childhood shows the man,
As morning shows the day.

— *John Milton*

After beginning recovery, we look back to reassemble the pieces of our life from a new perspective. It's like coming to an overlook on a mountain trail after hours of trudging upward through forest. We reach an opening on the edge of a cliff, the landscape falls away at our feet, and our view opens up. We look down over thousands of acres, and we can trace the trail below that we followed to get here. The simple questions are important: "Where did I come from?" "What route did I follow to get here?"

Integrating Who We Were with Who We Are

Many men put their mothers and fathers, sisters and brothers in the same box in which they stored their high school memorabilia — they're interesting to look back on, but they don't have much relevance to life today. One man said, "When I think about myself in my family as I grew up, I have a distant feeling that it's somebody I was once. I feel absolutely no connection or flow from who I was then to who I am now. It's like we're talking about two totally different people."

The breach in this man's history left me with an empty feeling. I wondered how he could ever have any relationship with himself, not to mention a feeling of self-esteem, if he could not integrate who he was in the past with who he is today. We are never the very same person today that we were yesterday. Yet, we need a sense of continuity. The man I was has shaped and educated the man I am now. The people I grew up with, who nurtured and fought with me, are part of the alloy at the core of my identity. No one can start from scratch at age twenty-one to create an adult self.

We first met the human world in our families. From their ways, they showed us how to be persons. Out of our family relationships, we learned how to be close and intimate, how to deal with conflict and resolve it, and how to regard ourselves as worthwhile. But learning and shaping our personalities never stops, even though what we learned in childhood about becoming a person affects all that we learn afterward. Recovery is about guiding and redirecting this continuing process to fulfill our potential and our value as men.

In recovery, we never completely start over. We reshape, remold, build on what we learned before. We came into the world as bundles of potential, overflowing with curiosity and an enthusiasm to learn. Virginia Satir used to say, "A child cannot not learn — and parents cannot not teach." Most of what a child is taught and learned in families happens by observation and by simply living in a family. In the same way, we learned our own name by hearing others use it to talk to us. We also developed our self-image by bumping up against the people and the challenges around us. Starting as babies with no sense of being anyone at all, we breathed in the images others had of us as we drew the breath of life. We learned to make distinctions between who we were and who we were not

— to feel we were lovable or worthless, strong or weak, male or female, tall or short.

As we learned to speak the language we heard around us, and not a foreign language, we also learned to get close or keep our distance from other people in our families. We learned from experience what we could and what we could not talk about in our families. We learned how to get together with others, how to express our feelings or hide them, how to eat, how to get comfort, and how to deal with touch, affection, and physical contact.

We simply absorbed all of this learning as little boys, eating and sleeping, being touched, and interacting. Only a small part of what we know was taught directly. So, we learned without knowing we learned, and we naturally continue to use our knowledge without thinking about it until it gets pulled from the well of our minds and identified as something we learned. Until it gets noticed, an action, an attitude, or a habit may seem normal, whether it is or not.

There is a story about a king of France in the Middle Ages who believed French was the natural language and all children would spontaneously speak it if they were not taught another language. To prove it, he took a baby boy away from his parents and, to let him develop his own speech, forbade the caretakers to speak in the presence of the child. Of course, the child didn't learn to speak at all since he didn't hear a language spoken, but he probably thought that was normal.

We all use our own experience to define what is normal, and sometimes we take very destructive, negative behavior for granted because we know no alternative. In recovery, we need to stand at the "overlook" to review our experiences and reconsider our definitions of normal and natural. Just as every individual has a unique set of fingerprints, every family has a unique pattern of communication, of celebrating, of grieving, and a history of specific events that changed its course. When we go back to look at our family patterns, we see that what we learned as children is only one way of responding to the world. We see that there are other options and directions we still can choose for our development — ones we could not even imagine before we reached this overlook.

"I didn't know how to express . . . any feeling . . ."

Dale gave up drugs when he was twenty-seven. When I talked to him about his recovery, he told me he knew for a long time before quitting that he was chemically dependent. He said, "But I figured, so what! It works for me." As his drug use continued, however, he got less and less out of it. He grew depressed and thought he would like to die. After one big weekend of doing tequila, mushrooms, and marijuana, and still feeling just as bad as when he wasn't using anything, he decided he had to quit.

In therapy, Dale remembered something from when he was eleven. He and a buddy had gone to a movie one evening, and afterward they stopped at a cafe for a burger. While eating, Dale looked up and saw his dad in another booth, kissing and caressing a strange woman. He immediately felt like vomiting and put his burger down. He told his friend he felt sick and had to go home. They paid the tab and walked home, but he didn't utter a word to his buddy about what he had seen. When Dale told his therapist about that event, it was the first time in his life he ever told anyone. He said, "When that happened, I didn't know what to do about it. I couldn't tell my mom because I knew they'd get a divorce. I didn't dare talk to my dad about it, so I just shut up."

When I said to Dale, "That must have been terribly painful to you as an eleven-year-old," a puzzled look settled on his face.

Trying to recall how he felt, he said, "I didn't know how to express pain, sadness, anger, or any feeling, so basically I did nothing."

The pattern of communication in Dale's family was to avoid all feelings. Avoiding feelings was what he learned about how to be a person and how to be with others. When flooded with powerful feelings at age eleven, he had no preparation for dealing with them. He didn't know what they were, how to express them, or how to get help from anyone. As he looked out over the trail he had followed, he reflected, "That's about when I started drinking, and not too long afterward I started smoking dope. I was the youngest of four kids and the biggest cutup in the family. Everybody was mad at me for being such a rebellious teenager. I didn't know why I was doing it. I just wanted to be away from home as much as I could and get smashed."

The Relief of Taking an Adult Look

When I review my family of origin, with an adult's awareness, I see a living system that has patterns. With this view, I am less judgmental of myself and less likely to unconsciously repeat the self-defeating patterns that may have troubled my father and his father.

In Dale's story, he thought his teenage use of chemicals and his addiction were signs that he was a bad kid. But, when he looked at himself in the context of a family system, he understood he was one member of his family expressing family pain. His loyalty to a nonexpressive, abusive family system shaped his silent and self-abusive behavior.

Dale's loneliness and self-abuse with chemicals interfered with his development as an emotionally healthy male, but it fit with what he learned about how to be a person in the midst of overwhelming challenges. He experienced betrayal by his father, but that was not the whole story. No one in his family was equipped to deal with feelings when they arose. Therefore, as an eleven-year-old, Dale was overwhelmed with feelings, and, at the same time, was alone because he couldn't talk about them. He was a child in an emotional trap.

Even if Dale gradually learned to live with and work around the trap as an adult man, the trap would have power over him and restrain his growth until he returned to break its grip. Years later, when people hear about a dark secret a person has kept since childhood, they often ask, "Why didn't you tell someone?" These people don't realize that when the adults don't talk about their strong feelings in a family, a child can't invent new family rules. He or she couldn't speak French if it wasn't spoken, regardless of how natural it might seem to someone else.

Dale was alone because he was speaking the language and following the rules of his family. In order to talk about what he saw, he would have to break the family rule against talk. Then he would have to invent a way to do it because it hadn't been modeled for him in intimate relationships. Obviously, he also would have risked recrimination or abuse. He was being the kind of person he was taught to be within his family system. All of this didn't make him an addict, but chemical use certainly fit like a glove with the pattern of his family system. It provided a way to cover his feelings and allowed him to remain loyally silent.

Not until Dale took an adult look at his family of origin could he see that many of his life problems were based on things he learned in his family. He always felt lonely and cut off from others in his family, that something was wrong with him, and that perhaps others in his family just didn't like him. When he learned about his family system, he discovered that loneliness was a pattern for everyone in the family. It was a family without a center. As a child he felt he wasn't part of the inside group, but no one was. Putting his memories in the context of his family system gave him a greater understanding of what was going on. He said, "When I realized that I wasn't lonely alone, it was a relief. I felt verified. It was then much easier for me to talk to my brothers and sisters."

How to Do Family of Origin Work

Fifteen years ago my partner and cotherapist, Rene Schwartz, and I developed an intensive family of origin workshop. It was designed to help budding family therapists explore and understand their own families as systems. The intensity and power of that workshop impressed us so much that we developed it further. We have repeated it every year since. So far, over two hundred people in groups of ten to fifteen each year have completed the course, and we have accumulated an immense amount of data about family of origin study. What began as a workshop for family therapists in training quickly grew to include nontherapists who wanted to study their families of origin.

Traditional psychotherapy encourages people to learn how their minds work by relying on memory and reflection. In contrast, family of origin study encourages people to go beyond their memories and reflections to talk directly with the people who are a part of their family systems, and to develop an adult perspective on their childhood. It's a method of

- reconsidering what you remember and what you thought was normal,
- getting additional facts to fill in missing pieces,

- uncovering family secrets that may have shaped you without your awareness, and
- opening new alternatives to continue your development.

Your memory and reflections are your clues and starting points, but the real work starts when you discuss your family with family members, old family friends, and distant relatives. The goal is to create a description of how your family system works, the rules for relationships that it passes down through the generations, and how it shapes its members.

Looking at the Whole Picture

If you think about how a person looks at a picture, it will help describe how family of origin study works. Normally, when we look at a picture, our eye naturally lands on the object in the foreground. Although we don't focus on the background, it is there, nonetheless, to tell part of the story. The subject of a picture might be a beautiful trout jumping in a stream. When viewed with the background of mountain peaks, a grassy meadow beside the stream flooded in sunshine, and a person standing upstream in waders, casting a line into the blue, frothy water, the trout becomes part of a story. To say it's a picture of a trout jumping would be true, but the whole story is told by seeing it in context.

If I am in the foreground in my own life picture, then my family is in the background. I can see and learn a great deal when I move my focus off myself and look at what my family in the background can tell me. Then, I see how the whole picture fits together. Of course, I will get nowhere if I approach it as a way to blame someone else for my troubles. But if I am looking for a way to understand and simply describe what is in the picture, new possibilities open up.

Kenny and His Dad

Rene Schwartz often uses the example of a small boy who has only limited awareness that other forces or dynamics exist beyond his experience. This boy, Kenny, is outside playing with other children. Another boy knocks him down, and Kenny runs home to tell his father. The father responds by adding his own attack on Kenny. He says, "You Little Chicken Shit. Don't come running home to me when a guy hits you. Go back out there now and hit him back. Don't come home until you do!"

With Kenny's limited circle of awareness, he feels like something must be wrong with him to have so disappointed his father. He has no way of knowing that his father and mother are in the midst of a conflict, and that his father feels angry and confused for not knowing how to talk with her. He doesn't know that his father went through the same experiences with his father and was treated in almost the same way as a child. Now, out of unconscious loyalty, Kenny's father is trying to be a good father by doing what his father did to him. He never challenged his loyalty to an unjust family system, so he passes it on to his son. Still, all young Kenny knows is that Dad disapproves of him.

As an adult, Kenny could be aware of much more. He could talk to his father and ask adult questions to examine the context in which his self-image developed. There are many ways to go back. It might happen quite naturally in families when the generations have open relationships with each other and are free to talk about the past. But often communication isn't open, or blocks develop between family members.

Talking Your Way to Understanding

In the family of origin workshop, we ask people to talk directly to their fathers and mothers, sisters and brothers, uncles, aunts, and cousins to assemble a description of their family as a system. It is a big job, but it is an effective way to take on the power of adulthood. You will deepen your knowledge of yourself and increase your self-acceptance. These strengths will spill over into the current close relationships in your adult life — your primary love relationship, father-child relationships, friendships, and work relationships. Once, you needed to leave your family to grow up and become emancipated. Now, you are going back into your family as an adult to continue your growth.

Sometimes one or all of the people from the original family are dead. But there's usually someone to talk with — old family friends, neighbors who lived next door, Dad's best buddy, Mom's confidante, an old aunt who can provide information and recollections about how the family operated. This is an adventure to pursue and often better than reading a good mystery.

To do this project, you need a way to organize the overwhelming amount of information you might find. We ask people in the family of origin workshop to organize their work into three kinds of data:

- a *family tree* that goes back at least three generations prior to your own,
- a *family life chronology* that lists major family events by year, and
- a list of the family's implicit *rules of interaction*.

Family Tree

The family tree should arrange each generation on its own limb and include dates of birth, death, and marriage for each family member. You can draw lines between people that display genetic and marital relationships; color code certain themes you want to trace such as alcoholism, a professional choice that runs in your family, or other themes that may interest you.

Family Life Chronology

The family life chronology is a list of major family events listed in chronological order. It should begin at least as early as the marriage dates of your grandparents and include all the comings and goings of individuals, marriages, job changes, deaths, family moves, house fires, fortunes won and lost, and major national events or community events such as wars, assassinations, floods, and earthquakes. This list provides a context to view your birth and development in your family and the flow of events in your family's life, some of which you will recall, some you won't. Where many major events occur in close succession — for example, two deaths and a job change in a year — the family system is under stress to incorporate the transitions constructively.

Rules of Interaction

The family rules of interaction are your own conclusions and interpretations. These are based on your experience collecting the information, what happened when you asked about sensitive topics, and the way your family dealt with significant events in the past. Summarize the patterns with simple rules of behavior. Some examples of family rules are:

- Never talk about the dead.
- Always do what pleases the women.
- Don't bring a discussion to a conclusion.
- Do what looks good at all costs.
- Avoid conflict.

When you have developed a list of family rules, you can see how you are following those rules, and how you would like to change them.

Try to Be Objective

In developing these three documents, you may be tempted to slant your search by looking only for the dirty stuff or only the glory in your family. If you have a backlog of unresolved anger about old injustices that you still want repaired, this is not the way to work on it. If you are trying to change your family or get them to be a healthier group, this is not going to help. The purpose is to give yourself more options by learning about the patterns you learned for intimate relationships.

Many people ask, "What would I talk about if I went to my parents or other family members to work on this project?" The guiding principle is to have a meaningful conversation about the real things in your life and theirs, or in your family's memories. Many families have these kinds of conversations with each other quite naturally. They simply reveal their personal responses, thoughts, and feelings to each other in the course of their conversations. If you already have that with your family, you have a rich resource for your growth. It may seem like an insignificant beginning to have a social contact when what you have in mind is "the big PERSONAL GROWTH." But an informal social visit, when you talk about important and unimportant events in your lives, might be an excellent beginning.

Once you've made contact, there are specific subjects that are useful to explore. They are the *universal* things that all people in all families deal with. But even though they are universal, some families live with "no-talk" rules that make them seem shameful or hard to speak about. Gathering the information about your family's experiences might sound like a dry, boring process, but it never is. It is often a wonderful, tender time of talking about fundamental family experiences. Nothing pleases most parents more than to have their children interested in their lives. It may also be a tense time because basic facts can be part of family secrets, or they may raise unsettled old issues that are still painful to discuss.

What follows is an outline of universal human issues all families deal with. It provides a format for exploring the patterns of your family system over generations. Using it will help you collect information for your family tree, family life chronology, and your list of family rules of interaction. After that is an outline of some dehumanizing and destructive processes many family patterns fall into, and an outline of enhancing and strengthening family processes you can look for in your family.

UNIVERSAL FAMILY EXPERIENCES

Birth

Gather dates, parents' names, who was present at the birth, and information about any adoptions. Include all still births and miscarriages.

Death

List dates, causes, who was present at the death, and how grief was handled. Was grief discussed? What issues arose about inheritances? How did the family come together following the death?

Other Comings and Goings of People in the Household

List stepparents, step siblings, grandparents, friends, lovers, et cetera. List dates, reasons, and subsequent reactions to the comings and goings.

Marriages

List dates for parents, grandparents, uncles, and aunts. Assemble courtship stories if you can. How did the first meeting occur? What were the initial attractions between the couple? Did their parents and other family members encourage the relationship?

Sex and Sexuality

How does touch occur? In what ways is sex talked about in the family? Is it affirmed? Enjoyed? Laughed at? Discussed exploitively or abusively? What permission is given to be sexual? What is considered an infraction of physical privacy and boundaries?

Emancipation

Gather the dates and ages that each young adult first left his or her parents' home. For what reasons did the person leave? Could the person come home again to live if needed? What reverberations occurred in other family relationships as a result of the person leaving home?

Relationships

Who was and is close to whom? Who fights with whom? Who confides in whom? What coalitions exist? Do siblings trust and confide in each other? Can people of different generations be open with each other? Do adults remain emotionally responsible so children can depend upon them? (Coded lines can be drawn on the family tree to display conflictual, close, and coalition relationships.)

Partnership and Battle of the Sexes

What privilege goes with femaleness in the family? With maleness? What power goes with each sex? What jobs? What respect or disrespect? Are there coalitions or shared experiences exclusively for males? For females?

DEHUMANIZING AND DESTRUCTIVE
FAMILY PROCESSES

Ungrieved Losses and Unresolved Grief

Learn about deaths and other losses that people never fully recovered from, or that they never discussed. These ungrieved losses can lead to people feeling distant, aloof, and cut off from other family members, and therefore less able to cope with subsequent change.

Cut-off Relationships

Gather information about discontinued relationships, or long silences, or signs that people dealt with pain or stress by creating distance.

Family Secrets

List events or pain that were kept secret. Secrets preserve family shame.

Addictions and Abuses

List the people involved in addiction or abuses of any kind and how it affected other family members. Sometimes these conditions are obvious, but families often look past them as if they don't exist or don't count. When you find them, their patterns reveal much about family dynamics and pain.

Family Isolation

Gather information on how your family includes friends and makes them part of family life. A family with close friends who they can bring into their home, socialize with, celebrate with, and share burdens with has a healthy support system. When families are isolated, no friends are invited in, friendships are limited or nonexistent. It is a symptom of family distress.

Childhood Abandonment and Neglect

Learn about child care and attachment patterns in your family. They often are repeated through generations.

ENHANCING AND STRENGTHENING FAMILY PROCESSES

Griefs and Losses Faced

Ask people in your family to tell you about some difficult events your family faced and write how they were handled. Confronting and dealing with hardship can be enhancing and bring out the best in people.

Openness and Acceptance of Differences

Learn about how your family handles diversity and differences within the family, and in the rest of the world. When people disagree, they can learn from each other. When a family member is different because of lifestyle, race, or disability, the difference can enrich the whole family.

Life Transitions Are Observed and Celebrated

Gather information about how your family marks important occasions, both joyful and sorrowful. Birthdays, anniversaries, bar mitzvahs, confirmations, weddings, and holidays are occasions for a family to gather and celebrate relationships. Funerals and other endings are observed as important times to gather and mark life changes.

Role Reliability and Flexibility

Gather information on roles that have persisted in your family, and how these roles are or are not flexible. Individuals in a family often have roles and jobs that they can be counted on to perform. Yet others sometimes step into those roles for respite, for fun, or for variety. For example, Mom can be counted on to be an active mother and Dad to be an active father, but they don't necessarily have rigidly held rules about what job each should or should not do.

"I guess there's no point in holding this back from you . . ."

My client, Don, was at his parents' home completing a family tree as part of his therapy. I had asked him earlier what part of his pain was inherited from his family, and what part was a direct product of his own life experience. Talking with his parents, he was gathering information about his family system in search of sources of his pain.

In this visit, he only asked questions about universal life issues. He didn't know a question he asked his mother about his grandparents' marriage date was loaded with feelings. He told me the next day that when he asked the question, she blanched white. Then, she glanced upward impulsively, as if to get permission from her dead mother to break their half-century-old pact never to reveal the truth. "Well, Don, I guess there's no point in holding this back from you. Grandpa Keely was really my step-father. He and Grandma got married when I was nine years old, and that's when we moved to Chicago. She was never married to my real father, and I never knew him. Until she married Grandpa Keely, Grandma and I lived in a small town in Wisconsin. We were extremely poor and sometimes all we had to eat was potatoes. Life was very hard until I was nine. My mother never talked about my real father, except one time she said he was a 'handsome liar.' After Mama and Daddy got married, we buried all that shame and left it in Wisconsin. I took the last

name Keely, and Mama told me never to tell my new
friends and schoolmates that Daddy was not my real
father."

Suddenly, Don had a great amount of information about
the unspoken pain of his mother's childhood. He had the
background for his mother's comments in his youth that "men
are untrustworthy" and "men are heroes." She had both kinds
of fathers. He also understood why she had been so fearful in
his youth about his developing sexuality and its potential to
create painful, tragic problems. Don's first reaction was imme-
diate empathy for his mother and the new details about her
childhood. They felt a rapport open between them and had a
discussion like they had not known in years. In the weeks and
months after, Don felt liberated by the details of his family
secrets. He felt relaxed about his choices for his life, free of the
burden of a vague perfectionistic standard, and free to make
mistakes.

**Mixed Emotions about Exploring
Your Family System Are Normal**

Men exploring their family system naturally swing between excitement and resistance. A man may be full of enthusiasm at first: it is exciting to embark on the adventure of a new
dialogue with one's family. He has a list of people he plans to
talk to and can't wait to get started. Several weeks later he
may say, "I spoke to my dad and mother one weekend and
two uncles the following week. They gave me a ton of information. But, suddenly this project looks absolutely huge to
me." That's where his excitement may turn to resistance, and
he may say, "Do you realize that what you are asking of me
could amount to a full-time job? I am overwhelmed and I've
lost my energy for this thing."

A man's emotional response may also go in the opposite direction. Having to talk to someone in his family about a specific issue — perhaps about a death that was never discussed, or an old conflict that was never finished — may be the last thing on earth he wants to do. The family rule against talking about it makes him feel sluggish. In his resistance, he creates rationalizations that the whole idea of studying his family is silly.

Finally, his friends push him into going anyway; so he does, and he raises the dreaded issues. In the midst of the discussion, the other family member tentatively opens up, and so does he. To his surprise, he becomes totally engrossed. When he leaves, he feels wonderful about the new connection that occurred between himself and the family member. Now, he is launched on new energy and a deep sense of awe about his project. He went from resistance to excitement.

Don't Try to Do It Alone

Because encountering the wall of resistance is almost inevitable, and because no one is objective about his own family system, it is essential that someone from outside the family help you decide which stones need to be turned over in the family story, and what directions to take. Everyone needs help to stay on track, and help raising questions that simply don't occur to you from within your family system's set of rules.

In the family of origin workshop, we arrange for mutual support by dividing people into small groups. They meet regularly to discuss their findings, their difficulties, and the issues they are exploring. They get ideas from one another about family patterns that are appearing, and they get the all-important support to confront the most difficult tasks. Most people in the workshop agree that, although they did all the work themselves, they never would have finished it without the group support and the structure to lead them.

Ways to Get Support

Another way to get the necessary support for this project is to do it as part of psychotherapy with the aim of becoming a separate individual within your family — to have emotional contact while maintaining your integrity as a full-grown man. If our reactions to our family are automatic, with no awareness of our choices, we feel controlled and want to blame our family. We may think, *Since my reactions seem automatic, my family is in control because they trigger them.* As long as we blame our family for our feelings and reactions, we keep ourselves in the child position. And if we break contact and choose to stay cut off from them, we freeze a large part of our emotional development and get stuck in the adolescent position. To become a separate adult and to keep relationships alive with one's family is the primary aim.

More Than a Family of Origin

We can have several kinds of families besides our family of origin, and I think it's healthy to have them. We may also be biological fathers or stepfathers to other children. We may have a family of friends we have chosen who play and relax with us, support us, share in our recovery journey, and celebrate important occasions with us.

The more we learn how to maintain our integrity without resorting to blaming others for our troubles, while staying in emotional contact with our families, the less difficulty we will have with all relationships and stress.

What Is an Enmeshed Family System?

Sometimes a man is so woven into his family's outlook on life and so involved in taking care of them or being taken care of, that all of his emotions are, at their root, reactions to other family members. He might say, "When you're happy, I'm happy. When you're sad, I'm sad." He is unable to have a rational thought except when everyone else is calm. That family system is called *enmeshed*.

The opposite of enmeshment looks different, but produces some of the same results. In this case, a man may have tried to escape the feeling of being too close, or too controlled, so he cuts off all emotional connection. Some cut off families have no contact with each other for years. Other families see each other rather routinely, but never talk about real things that have emotional content.

The real things might be a guy's worry that his girlfriend is losing interest in him, or that his last child's first day of kindergarten is a big milestone in his own life, or that his boss has been giving him high praises at work. Cut-off relationships don't support men's natural development into stronger manhood because they avoid issues completely. If you're not faced with the issue, you can't learn from it. A man cut off from his family either stays isolated from emotional contact, or, where he is in contact with a spouse or friend, he is so dependent that he doesn't function at an adult level.

In family therapy, we coach a man to make emotional contact, to get beyond the family rule barriers and talk about the real issues in his own life and his family members' lives. He consciously works to develop true emotional contact with them, without losing himself. He may need new skills for relationships based on respect and affirmation, rather than getting together around victim-victimizer interaction, caretaker-controller responses, or joining around negativism and depression. He has to learn in a hundred different ways that when someone pitches him the ball, he can choose to swing at it or to let it go by.

Nothing raises emotional issues out of the pool of denial onto the surface of a man's awareness like bringing his family of origin relationships into his current life. Any of us can talk with confidence and authority about the real character of our fathers or mothers when we reflect from the safety of our own minds. If our ideas about them never have to match reality, we can stay relaxed in our protected cocoon, remaining un- changed in our beliefs about them. But, inviting one's family to talk about real-life history can quickly turn one's bravado, self-pity, or self-satisfaction into a case of jelly legs and uncer- tainty. But we ought to seek this kind of vulnerability because it creates openings for change and growth.

The benefits people get from immersing themselves in this work are rich and far-reaching. A man often feels he has found his family again after this kind of work. Many men have said, "I feel like I know my father as a person for the first time, and I love him." These men gain a sense of participation in the flow of generations, a feeling of being part of the great power of family, and more choice about which patterns to continue and which to change.

CHAPTER 6

Relationships:
Love Transforms the Lover

I feel the more I know God,
that He would sooner we did wrong in
loving then never love for fear we should
do wrong.
                                    -- Father Andrew

Loneliness is an undercurrent in many men's lives. They are good-hearted, caring, and loving people. Yet their relationships feel distant or troubled because of loyalty to the myth that achieving something alone is better than achieving it with help or cooperation. Many learn to live with loneliness as a fact of life. They even become numb to it. But the cost remains high. Chronic loneliness is not normal; it's not healthy and it is painful.

When a man first decides to change direction in his life he needs to take note of how he conducts his relationships. He needs the healing power of love and he must learn how to become available to it. He is like a guy with a backpack carrying all his accumulated experiences, beliefs, and habits. He can't simply toss the whole pack aside when he takes a new path. He has to unpack and see what he has collected, then decide what to keep and what to discard. Large parts of his baggage are filled with all the relationships, friendships, and family ties he's had for years. Changing his path may require discarding unhealthy myths that say he should not depend on others, he should be self-sufficient and invulnerable.

All people are dependent on others. We have no more choice about it than we have about breathing. We can either be honest about our dependency and engage in healthy, loving, interdependent relationships, or we can be dishonest by pretending not to need others. We can even get a false high from our dishonesty, a sense of power, an exciting feeling of invincibility, a feeling of total self-control — an ego trip in which we say, *I'm powerful. I don't need anybody.* Ultimately, such defiant dishonesty leads to great problems in our lives. We may even become covertly overdependent on a person and not realize it.

Getting Honest about Dependency

Milder forms of denying dependency are when an isolated man says, *I'm doing just fine without close friends.* He may have come to accept his loneliness as a normal fact of life, so it no longer registers as pain. He adjusts to it and may even say, *It wouldn't feel natural for me to try to make friends. If it happened naturally, that would be fine, but I don't want to be phony about it.* His rationalization helps him avoid the awkwardness and the risk of learning the social skills to reach out. Becoming personal or friendly may feel unnatural because it's unfamiliar. In the same way, if I were to suddenly try to run the high hurdles, it would feel awkward. I probably wouldn't be very good at it. But if I had been doing it every day, every move would feel natural. Sometimes healing requires discomfort and unfamiliar behavior, abandoning "normal," familiar feelings.

Some Misconceptions about the Word "Love"

My understanding of "love" has changed and expanded over the course of my recovery and growth. As a child, I learned about the different kinds of love: platonic love — the affection between two friends or buddies; romantic or erotic love — sexual attraction and desire; familial love — the affection and attachment between parents and children, brothers and sisters. But I always had a feeling that the word *love* had a special and intense meaning.

Whenever I heard about the power of love to heal, to change the world, to transform us, I didn't think of the ordinary, everyday relationships I already had in my life. Hearing popular love songs made me expect an ecstatic feeling with love, not the comfort of everyday contact. I thought love was a feeling that rose powerfully within us and was always easy to identify the moment we felt it. It seemed magical, mystical, powerful, and intimate especially in romance. I got the impression the word ought to be sung by a chorus to convey its full meaning, not spoken in ordinary words. Therefore, love seemed remote from my daily experience. I knew love was part of my life, and sometimes I was deeply moved by feelings of connection, but the word *love* remained an intangible, sometimes a bit too sweet, and I didn't have a gut-level understanding of it.

The Power of Love Is Shown in Relationships

My understanding has changed. I have learned that the power of love to transform our lives is actually in all of our relationships. It's often not ecstatic, and there are far more than three or four kinds of relationships. Some are deep, intimate, lifetime partnership commitments, such as a marriage. Some are caring friendships. Some are casual acquaintances with people we see occasionally in our neighborhood, at our children's school, or at work. Some relationships are based on mutual participation in community or a group such as a synagogue, a church, a school, a self-help group, a Twelve Step meeting, a service club, a bowling team, or a sports club. In these situations, the umbrella of the group, the spirit of community, and the regularity of seeing each other weekly year after year can create bonds of true attachment between people — even if they have never discussed anything deeply personal. All of these kinds of relationships carry the power of love that transforms and heals.

Are They Saying, "Men Should be Different?"

It isn't only men in crisis who carry the baggage of loneliness. Many writers and observers note the isolated and alienated condition of men in general. Psychologist and writer Stuart Miller writes with a mournful tone in his book, *Men & Friendship*.

> After all, what is "a man" nowadays? Somebody who stands alone, independent of all ties. A man is supposed to give up his callow buddies in late adolescence or in his twenties, to get a job, to get married, to get serious. If something seems missing in his life, he is supposed to forget about it, to be stoical about his disappointments. Our society seems to say that a real man needs and wants nobody — except maybe a woman. And even she can be temporary.[1]

Jan Halper, Ph.D, interviewed 4,126 men in positions of management and professionals, spending one hour with each of them, and wrote a book she called *Quiet Desperation*. She observes:

> Few [men] have opened up to their wives or talked to one another about intimate feelings. Instead they have handled their inner turmoil in the proper male fashion, stoically and silently. So they have suffered inside. . . . Men are cut off from who they are. They have been taught to deny their inner world, to avoid their feelings, to live according to prescribed ways of being.[2]

Theologian James B. Nelson writes in his book *The Intimate Connection*:

> Indeed, we who are men do seem to handle our lives with an activity-and-achievement style, we handle others with a style of dominance and submission, and we handle our psyches with a style that prizes logical cool levelheadedness. None of these characteristics is particularly conducive to nurturing the capacities for intimacy and friendship.[3]

These observations are only a sample of many similar comments published in recent literature on men's issues. I have two reactions every time I come across one of them. Part of me says, *Yes, I can see what they are talking about.* Another part of me feels defensive for our gender and I say, *Hey! What about appreciating the good side of men's relationships?* What about valor and honor and loyalty and men's readiness to be courageous, to sacrifice, to be heroic under extreme conditions? What about the man in the airliner that crashed into the river in Washington, D.C., several years ago? He calmly and lovingly helped many people out of the sinking plane and onto the rescue helicopter while he was still tangled in his seat belt. Instead of saving himself, he rescued those around him and was pulled under and drowned as the plane slowly sank. Aren't there masculine qualities to celebrate and write about? Aren't there qualities we can admire in men's relationships?

Yes, there are. And no doubt the writers and observers of men's issues are keenly interested in advancing the well-being of men. Yet, their comments have the ring of truth and perhaps that's what gets under my skin. I recognize myself and my friends in their descriptions, and it doesn't feel good. The writers seem to be saying, "Men should be different!"

These writers' observations of men's problems with relationships also ring true from another perspective. As a therapist, I don't meet men in general; I encounter them one at a time in my office, as they "awaken" in therapy. In that situation, a man does not ask in detached intellectual tones, "Why do men tend to be so cut off from other people in their lives?" He is in anguish as the truth of his circumstance crashes in on him. He doesn't speculate on the strange foibles of men who stay alone. He feels trapped, perhaps even suffocated. He may be ashamed of his loneliness and sees no options for himself. His isolation feels like a condition, not a choice or a defense. Henry David Thoreau said that "The mass of men lead lives of quiet desperation." Suddenly, the man getting in touch with himself, who is waking up, is no longer quiet in his desperation. He might be able to heroically rise to the occasion in a crisis like the man did in the airliner crash. But to sustain a private, personal connection with another person over time may make him feel like he is all thumbs.

". . . my helmet was in the sights of somebody's rifle . . ."

A career military man, Tom, came into therapy because his wife found out about his extramarital affair, and he wanted to avoid messing up his life even more. As we looked at the emotional stresses he had faced, he felt the impact of his experiences for the first time. He had been in combat in Vietnam and told me in detail about going out on patrol. For the first time, he described the terror he felt one dark night crossing a meadow under rifle fire. He said, "I saw the tracer bullets flying just an inch above my head — I don't have words to describe the feeling I got when I suddenly realized — my helmet was in the sights of somebody's rifle, and he pulled the trigger to get me." He began to sob as he described the absolute desperation that surged within him as a teenager in battle and his frantic mental search to find a way out of combat duty.

Tom hadn't talked with anyone about it. Not his wife, not any friends. I asked him to put all the details into words for me because details recapture one's emotional responses. He described the way the sky looked from the jungle floor. He recalled the morning routine in camp. And he remembered the look on the face of the dead soldier with the mangled, bloody body he had to spend one long night with alone in a field.

The details brought back his feelings from the past and he reclaimed them. In the process, he also broke through his loneliness by letting me know what he felt. When this happens to a man, it is sometimes as if he doesn't realize how thirsty he is until he gets a drink of water.

Tom sobbed uncontrollably as it came rolling back into his memory. He was overwhelmed with new feelings, and it was a relief to have another man know exactly how he felt. It wasn't safe to talk when he packed away this baggage, but he could afford to let down now because it was safe. Some of his reactions were similar to any abused person who finally admits to himself what he has been through. He thought his flood of feelings was a sign of how crazy or disturbed he was. He said, "I feel like I'm falling to pieces," and it was frightening to him.

Actually, it was a sign of his capacity to grow and recover. I could only tell him that he wasn't falling to pieces, that he was inexperienced in letting his feelings rise to the surface and sharing them with someone, and that he didn't know how to handle them yet. I also told him that his feelings would come and go in waves, but that he wouldn't lose his ability to cope with life. I told him that he had known only how to be alone and hide his feelings. "You need more options than that. Now you're learning how to let someone into your experience so they can be with you," I told him.

Our Basic Nature as Men and as Human Beings Can be Found in Relationships

Our need for contact, for connection with people is woven into the fibers of our deepest nature. This need is so fundamental that a syndrome called *failure to thrive* develops in infants who fail to get the loving touch and interaction of other people. This has been seen in orphanages, in long-term hospital care, and in families with neglected children. Adequate personal contact and touch are essential to life for a child, or else he or she loses weight, becomes lethargic, and dies.

As we develop, we grow more separate, more capable of independence, and more able to nurture, protect, and care for children and the infirm around us. We may not be as dependent on others as when we were children, but our need for human contact never disappears. This was underscored by research published in the magazine *Science*. Three researchers — James House, Karl Landis, and Debra Umberson — summarized studies of more than thirty-seven thousand people who were followed for up to twelve years. The researchers found that social isolation "is as significant to mortality rates as smoking, high blood pressure, high cholesterol, obesity, and lack of physical exercise. . . . In fact, when age is adjusted for, social isolation is as great or greater a mortality risk than smoking." While smoking increases the risk of getting sick to 1.6 times normal, social isolation increases the risk of getting sick to twice the normal level. Furthermore, they found evidence that isolation is even more devastating to men than to women.[4]

The intense emphasis in our culture on individual rights, autonomy, and individual achievement can overshadow our basic relational nature. People have always found their nature and their fulfillment through their tribe, clan, family group, or nation. Individual achievement, heroism, and feelings of personal completeness were achieved through fulfilling the clan or tribe's needs, ideals, and goals, not through competing and getting ahead of others for personal gain.

Homophobia

Many heterosexual men's anxiety about avoiding any sign of homosexuality can drive them away from close friendships with other men. Many men seem to carry a cultural touchiness, afraid that anyone might think they are gay, or that another man's homosexuality might reflect badly on them. It's a neurotic anxiety called *homophobia*. Its destructive effects keep men isolated and insecure because it is through closeness with other males that masculine identity deepens and matures. Women tell me they don't generally carry the same burden of anxiety about the appearance of their sexual preferences. Stuart Miller describes what happened when he told people he wanted to write a book about men and friendship. He got many responses like, "Male friendship. You mean you're going to write about homosexuality? That's what everybody will think, at least. Could be dangerous for you." He writes, "Everywhere I have gone there has been the same misconception. The bizarre necessity to explain, at the beginning, that my subject is not homosexuality. . . . The only moving human relationships that people seem able to conjure up are erotic ones."[5]

Make a Choice for Relationships

The choice to give priority to personal relationships for their own sake puts a man out of the mainstream of American male culture. In a sense, men's renewal and recovery is an alternative lifestyle. Whether a man is recovering from chemical dependency, a divorce, or a physical illness, he needs internal strength and integrity, plus the support of his friends to follow his path. By making active choices rather than passively following the prescriptions and compulsions of the dominant culture, a man gets free to live a life of friendships, connection, and health.

The most visible signs of men on fire with the spirit of recovery are in the ways they make room for relationships in their lives. They break their "female dependency" by including other men as true friends. They set time aside and they call a male friend for lunch or dinner with no more reason than enjoying the company and conversation. This change toward a more relationship-oriented life takes many small steps for most men. Like anything else, we learn by experience how to give and receive more love in our lives.

We may feel awkward at first. We may need to literally force ourselves to suggest to another man, "How about meeting for lunch someday?" Or we may have to decide ahead of time that when we are golfing with a friend, we're going to find an opening to say something personal like, "My father is really ill and I'm upset about it." Or we may have to force ourselves to break tradition and call an old friend just to say hello and talk, even though we've never done it before.

In therapy, I often ask a man if he has any friends because friendship is a vital element in his healing. The man often replies, "My friends all live out of town," even when he has lived in this city for years. Such a man has obviously been surviving with sparse contact with his friends.

Another common reply is, "I had good friends when I was younger, and I still consider them my friends, but I don't talk to them more than once or twice a year."

One man said, "I felt for years that no one really knew me or what I was like inside. It made me so sad I cried about it sometimes. But hell, now I realize it's even worse than I thought! I'm even cut off from myself. I don't even know what I'm like inside half the time. And when I do know, I'd just as soon get rid of what I see."

A recovering man needs the renewal that relationships can provide to bring the transforming power of love into his life. He needs to become part of a vital, larger whole. For his strength, his health, and his competence, for endurance to ride through times of weakness and trouble, he needs what every person needs: both to give love and to receive it.

Love is never a fix. Rather, as we talk about love in this chapter, we mean a flow between people who care about each other. These are relationships and attachments that grow and develop over time, like a dialogue over years that gathers momentum and builds on itself. The dialogue of a relationship means playing together, facing life events and supporting one another through them, having misunderstandings and staying involved to work them out; it means sometimes being mistaken, or inadequate, or hurtful, and then accepting and giving forgiveness.

". . . we've talked through tough life issues; we've exposed our weaknesses . . . "

When I think about my friendship with my friend Norm, I see our commitment to each other in that we make a point of getting together about once a month. We usually meet for dinner and simply talk and eat, and when it's time to leave we set a time for our next dinner together. Norm and I first met as eighteen-year-old college freshmen, living a couple of doors away in the same dormitory. Our relationship began as college guys having fun, talking about all the things that interest young men in college — like women and the philosophy of life. It continued as we each got serious in relationships with women, finished college, and went separate ways with our traveling, careers, and marriages. But we always re-established our connection with visits, telephone calls, or letters.

The early base we built of trust and honesty has rewarded us with the feeling that we can pick up where we left off each time we get together. Our relationship dialogue has sustained us through the twists and turns of many years: choosing spouses, marriage, children, serious illnesses in our families, divorce, career changes, doubts about ourselves, and emotional upheavals. Today our relationship is deepened by our history. But if we never talked about what was really happening in our lives, if we only talked about sports, politics, and the weather, we never would have deepened our relationship.

Norm and I have had fun together; we have each lived through tough life issues; we've exposed our weaknesses while we still didn't know which way to turn. We have admired each other's strength and integrity when choices were hard and excused each other's foibles. We both know from experience that no matter what, Norm is on my side and I am on his. He accepts me as I am. He doesn't try to change, improve, defeat, or use me for his gain, and I don't do that with him. That kind of knowing, beyond all facades, comes from always coming back to renew our connection.

Friendships and Other Connections

We need friends, we need intimate partners, and we need to be part of a community. We have families we were born into, and others that were born to us, where we can find intimacy. Others have families of "affiliation" that we gather around us for family-style relationships. Self-help groups such as Alcoholics Anonymous, Al-Anon, and others are examples. On a larger scale, we may also participate in neighborhood, school, church, or governmental events. Pride in a group, the feeling of being part of the larger whole, of being a participant in a community, heal and restore us.

For awhile, I attended the regular meetings of the city council in my hometown because I wanted to be involved in and informed about the affairs of my community. Although I was never a member of the city government, by just attending I felt a part of local events. It's surprising how a city council meeting can become like spontaneous theater when issues such as zoning ordinances and traffic signals get raised for decisions that affect neighbors' lives.

**The Difference between
Membership and Individualism**

Membership takes us beyond individualism; it means we have a place as part of something bigger than ourselves; it can satisfy a side of our nature that will never be fulfilled through individual, competitive achievement. At my church I've participated on maintenance committees, volunteered to usher at services, joined discussion groups and progressive dinners because that is how I participate as a member of a community.

Along with membership in a community comes participation in the lives of others. We don't live insulated existences, responding only to whatever happens directly to us. When a friend's mother dies it touches us, too, and we may need to lend support. When a friend gets married or his child graduates from high school, we may be part of the celebration. When life events occur directly to me, the community is there to uphold and be with me. Membership erodes the loneliness of isolation. And playing a part in others' tragic and happy events prepares us for similar transitions in our own lives.

Learning to Love Ourselves and Others

It is often said that to love someone, we must first love ourselves. Yet, I believe it is equally true that the more we feel love for and from other people, the more we learn to love ourselves. All kinds of love teach us about love.

We need to *learn* to love ourselves, and we can do that by making some choices. We can't choose to love ourselves, but we can choose to take a stance or an attitude toward ourselves. We can *act* like a loving friend, even if we don't *feel* deserving of it. We can choose to defend ourselves against unfair attacks, give ourselves honest appraisal and plenty of forgiveness, and take care of our physical and emotional needs. Acting in loving ways leads to feeling that way and teaches us to be more loving with our friends.

The Design of Healthy Relationships

Loving relationships are healthy relationships and they are a requirement for recovery. Some people define health as the absence of illness and look for defects or sickness to check for the presence of health. In human relations, this outlook creates perfectionism and considers any problem as unhealthy. But, problems are part of healthy human life; it's how we respond that determines whether a relationship is healthy or not.

When a man begins to emphasize relationships in his life, he may be picking up his development where he left off as a teenager. If so, he may feel again the inadequacies he felt at that age about being accepted and the anxieties about how he should act. Maybe he learned as a teenager how to avoid those feelings by getting into an addictive relationship with a chemical, or maybe an overly exclusive relationship with a woman, or by throwing himself into work, school, or achievement. In any case, a man choosing to emphasize relationships in his life is returning to his unfinished task of learning how to be a friend, a peer, a partner, a lover, a member. He is intentionally choosing to design a life with healthy relationships.

Living through the Discomfort

The first advice I have for a man at this point is to live through the discomfort of learning how to be in relationships. You will feel awkward and make mistakes, but you will get over them eventually. People learn necessary things from mistakes. Fumbling and awkwardness don't make us bad people; they happen to all learners. This is your turn to be a learner.

Reaching Out

Also, don't expect a quick change in your relationships the moment you decide to work on them. Relationships grow from experience and are built over time. Put yourself into positions where you will meet people. Go to Parents Without Partners, or a Great Books Club, or attend a church or synagogue if that meets your needs. Besides attending formal services, attend the classes they offer, or the social events. Go to the local library, school district, and local college to see what adult classes they offer in subjects that interest you. Karate classes, golf or racquetball classes, choirs and singing groups, writing classes, drama groups, and outdoor recreation experiences are also available in many communities. When you go, you will meet others there with interests similar to your own.

Many community service organizations need volunteers to provide such services as serving meals at shelters for the homeless, answering telephones for crisis hotlines and making referrals to community and government agencies, and being a driver for the disabled. These organizations offer many opportunities to meet people, to build relationships, and to contribute to the well-being of your community.

QUALITIES OF HEALTHY RELATIONSHIPS

The rest of this chapter will list specific qualities of healthy relationships as a guide for developing them. No words can substitute for the emotional vitality, the ecstacy and agony of a good friendship, a dynamic group, or a love affair. Words encourage us, they direct us, they shed light on what we have experienced, and they provide standards and goals, but they are no substitute for actual experience.

This list of relationship qualities is not the same as the wisdom of experience. You still have to do it, right and wrong, to learn it.

1. *Attachment*
This is the feeling of affection, care, and involvement that grows and builds between people over

time. It is one of the durable ingredients of friendships, marriages, family connections, and group relationships. As people get to know each other, as they simply share time and space in their lives, as they respond to mundane daily events, play together, work together, as they push against each other in conflicts, they make each other increasingly important in their lives.

Stuart Miller has written poetically about attachment. He writes, "As much as anything else, friendship is the inner habit of holding someone . . . in your heart."[6] Attachment grows by letting someone know us better, by expressing our reactions rather than screening them and exposing our spontaneous feelings.

In erotic relationships, the romantic idea of "falling in love" suggests something magical comes over us. Romantic love can be an exciting beginning to a love relationship, but it should never be mistaken for attachment. Erich Fromm says, "This idolatrous love is often described as the true, great love; but while it is meant to portray the intensity and depth of love, it only demonstrates the hunger and despair" that the person has brought with him to the relationship.[7] This feeling is very transitory.

Attachment grows deeper with two ingredients: time and familiarity. Most of us have had the experience of spending hours, days, even years with someone and still we felt we didn't really know them. This happens when a person never reveals spontaneous inner reactions. Such a person is so tightly wound, so guarded, that nothing is expressed until it's weighed and approved. More time with this person only ekes out the slightest bit more familiarity. Our task in recovery is to risk letting ourselves be known, to become transparent to our trusted friends, so our attachment can build on familiarity.

2. *Reliability*

This is the quality in a relationship that lets two people know they can count on one another to resolve tension and conflict, and to talk about misunderstanding. It's knowing that loving feelings will be accompanied by loving behavior, not abusive, degrading, or discounting behavior. An underlying feeling of trust, continuity, and constancy are part of a reliable relationship. It's knowing that the past connects with the present and whatever occurred in the past can be resolved to create a better present and future.

Reliability doesn't mean that people won't get angry or misunderstand, or that they won't ever hurt each other. It means they will be accountable for their actions. And it means they can see what is coming in one another's reactions and can feel some influence over each other. Our relationship with a friend is affirmed when we can count on certain things to make them angry, to make them laugh, or to touch their love.

Moodiness is the opposite of reliability. With moodiness, people can have a wonderful feeling of togetherness and openness one day, but the next day, for no apparent reason, the mood has shifted. Feelings of connection inexplicably change to emotional distance and aloofness. Then, people often try to decipher what hidden reason created the shift, and they "walk on egg shells" as if hidden land mines might go off at any moment. Such efforts are never a good use of anyone's energy.

In addicted and abusive families moodiness is commonplace and people think it's normal. To say, "I'm in a bad mood," somehow is supposed to explain a sudden change to negative, abusive, or withdrawn actions. Instead, it creates a climate of unpredictability. Even when feelings are warm and generous at a given moment, if a family system or relationship doesn't have reliability, there is little trust. People can't relax when feelings are good because there is a pattern of unpredictable mood shifts.

If connections are always in danger of being swept aside by a mood swing, then no deep trust can ever develop. People are always starting over again and, regardless of how long their relationships last, they never build beyond this tentative beginning.

Children in abusive families often describe the anger and punishment of their father or mother as coming without warning. They say, "We never knew what kind of mood he was going to be in at supper time. Sometimes he would be jovial and pleasant and sometimes, out of the blue, he blew up in a rage." In contrast, good discipline with children lets them know what is coming. In a reliable parent-child relationship, a father might say, "If you keep screaming and kicking the table, you will have to go to your room until you settle down." This provides a feeling of process and predictability. Events follow logically and a mood shift doesn't happen without warning or transition. In a reliable relationship, one is the same person in anger as in tenderness. A sense of fairness and justice in the relationship, whether in a love affair or in a parent-child relationship, flows from the experience of reliability, continuity, and accountability.

A recovering man must make connections between the various moments in his relationships. He must set aside defensiveness and talk about the discrepancies in his conduct noticed by his partner, his friend, or his child. And he needs to raise questions of others when the connections aren't clear to him. Many men, especially those who are used to unreliability in their relationships (which includes most of us to some degree), simply swallow their confusion and their questions.

Recovery demands that we talk about the transitions in our relationships and the discontinuity or confusion we feel. Talking fills the gaps, builds trust, and allows our relationships to grow more reliable. Naturally, we will not always want to face the tension in such discussions. But when we hold ourselves accountable without shaming ourselves, and when we do the same for others in our relationships, the tension is constructive, not hurtful or destructive.

3. *Faithfulness*

This word covers more aspects of a relationship than we often realize. In marriage, we often think faithfulness means no extramarital sex. In other relationships, we think being faithful means being loyal and conscientious, like a long-standing friend who offers support in crisis, or a caring son who maintains contact with his aged parents. In this sense, faithfulness refers to someone who stays true to the relationship and who keeps the faith during the hills and valleys created by life changes. Faithfulness means we continue to believe in our friendship, and our love, even when there is no contact to sustain it every minute. It means we keep returning to the inner knowing we have of the love, and the relationship agreement.

The model of faithfulness in friendship that I carry with me is with my friend Diane. Over the course of our friendship, she has kept contact even when I haven't. When my delusions told me my friendship didn't have much value to anyone, and when I was distracted by my own problems, she continued to affirm our connection. Diane would call, or arrange for our family to get together with her. She is not only my friend, but also my wife's and my children's friend. Part of her faithfulness is in her acceptance of us, regardless of what we are feeling or what is going on with us. One evening when we were together I said, "I guess I won't be very good company because I'm so tired." Her natural reply was, "So, go ahead and be tired. We can still have an evening together including your tiredness." That kind of faithfulness and acceptance seems to come out of her acceptance of herself.

In marriages where one member has been sexually un-faithful, both partners often have long-standing patterns of covert unfaithfulness. Both have ways of dropping the faith in their emotional connection to the other. Both tend to fail to affirm their bond. Both drop the ball when it's time to return to each other to complete or resolve an issue.

A recovering man, focusing on the quality of faithfulness, consciously practices affirming his connections. When no external signs say that connection exists, he doesn't wait for them or lament their absence — he creates them. He writes a letter, makes a phone call, brings a gift, expresses his feelings. When unfinished issues wait to be resolved, or tension needs to be discussed, he returns to them for completion. He accepts the unrewarding times in a relationship as part of the total picture.

4. *Conflict*

Conflict is necessary in a relationship because all human beings are different, and all have different senses of timing, of taste, of needs, and of desires. Conflict, when brought out into the open and re-solved, is nature's way of preserving relationships and deepening them.

My wife and I have recently redecorated our kitchen. She cares more deeply about the choice of curtains than I do, but I have strong feelings about the kind of floor covering we get. Conflict is intense engagement with each other and after twenty-seven years of marriage, we have had enough conflicts and resolved enough of them so that we have learned to appreciate each other's preferences. We don't always agree, but past conflicts now serve like an accumulated pool of knowledge about each other. When we went to buy the kitchen materials, we were surprised at how easy and efficient our disagreement and resolution process has become over the years.

Two important factors guide conflict in a relationship. One is openly expressing disagreement. The other is having techniques for resolving it after it comes up. Sometimes conflict is continuous and open but is never resolved. You can also sustain unresolved conflicts by never bringing them up for discussion or never admitting they exist. A man who feels his job is to be a peacemaker can get so skilled at avoiding conflict that he never knows it exists. When a couple tells me that they never disagree, I expect to find a great deal of hidden tension between them. The tension usually comes out indirectly as quiet resentment, as boredom with the relationship, as personal depression, and even as physical health problems.

The first step to resolving conflict is to bring it into the open. Accept disagreement as a fact of life. The second step is to work toward mutually respectful solutions. Most conflicts don't require agreement to be resolved, just a feeling by all concerned that their outlook is understood. The only way to get the benefit of conflict resolution is to take the risk and temporarily live with the discomfort created by honest disagreement. Honesty can carry one into a disagreement, and it can also carry one on to the resolution of it.

5. Separateness

Separateness within togetherness is essential to a healthy relationship. We often misunderstand the nature of love because of love songs and unrealistic romantic ideas about love. A relationship must not wipe out an individual's identity. The creation of a new relationship, whether a friendship or a marriage, creates a new entity, but it does not absorb the individuality of the people in the relationship.

In a relationship, the whole is more than the sum of its parts. A baseball team has morale or lacks it, and their morale is a force that affects how they play. It is beyond any one team member's control. Similarily, you can't predict how any two individuals will combine in a relationship because each relationship has its own morale, spirit, history, direction, and momentum.

Some people avoid the stress of separateness amid the spirit of togetherness. They try to have a good relationship by melting all individual differences and becoming one person. They swallow all disagreement or sidestep any acknowledgement of it. In truth, each is born separately, each has a separate life path, each will die alone. A healthy, loving relationship is a dialogue between people who accept their separate paths.

Codependency often is a way of emotionally denying separateness. Many men are codependent because they seek masculine fulfillment primarily by having a satisfied partner, wife, or lover. This focus on satisfying the other person is often related to men's idea of being a good man by being a good provider, and being a good man by being a satisfying sexual partner. A codependent man believes, *If my partner is happy, if she's satisfied, I must be okay as a person.* The man in such a relationship is continuously measuring his self-esteem by his partner's satisfaction, and becomes so attentive to her feelings that he loses sight of his own. This can propel men into supporting and encouraging a partner's lavish spending habits, unhealthy drinking, or other self-destructive or self-centered behavior.

6. *Risk*

Any loving connection includes risk. When we become attached to someone, we become vulnerable to them. As soon as we meet a new friend, we risk losing him or her. We know nothing is permanent, except change, and caring about other people means their changes will affect us. When my friend tells me he's considering a career move, I'm struck with the changing nature of life. I want him to have what he wants, but the change would be a personal loss to me.

To have a relationship at all, we must surrender ourselves to the risk of being known. When someone gets acquainted with my personal preferences, my taste in music, my passion for a certain type of candy bar, or when someone is with me when I fall on my face, I am vulnerable to that person. The risk of sharing these things provides possibilities for growing and possibilities for loss and hurt. But without risk, there are no possibilities.

Couples who come into therapy because of sexual disfunction sometimes know nothing about emotional nudity. They don't know about taking risks, exposing spontaneous feelings, or talking about sensitive, private memories. When in bed together, they are puzzled about their problems with physical intimacy; they don't realize that physical responses often follow emotional responses. Therapy in these cases often centers on coaching them to take off their emotional clothes with each other so they can risk emotional intimacy. The physical intimacy can more easily follow then.

I accept that there will be pain and disappointment in my relationships — even in the best of them. I can't be all I wish all the time. But in risking, I don't totally turn myself over to the mercy of another person. While I risk how another person will respond, I also have a right to basic respect and dignity. I will stand up for that and demand it from all of my relationships. I expect pain and imperfections, but I can continue to talk through it, or return later to resolve what is unfinished.

7. *Celebration*

This is an important part of a loving connection. Sharing all the special moments in life, such as a job promotion, the birth of a child, passing a test, completing a tough project, noting a child's graduation, bar mitzvah, or confirmation, all are worthy of major and minor celebrations. It might mean just a telephone call to say, "I did it!" Or, it might mean a dinner party and dancing. When we only pay attention to our problems and our work, we cannot build upon or expand those things we prize the most. These celebrations are positive affirmations that say, "Our connection is good and loving, and it sustains us."

Love and Relationships Transform Us

In the experience of loving and being loved, hope grows within us. Our self-centeredness is broken down. Attachment carries us beyond ourselves and spins a thread of continuity that spans the ups and downs and the gaps of space between our paths. The tangible experience of continuity between two people brings mystery and infinity into our daily lives. If we are willing or able to accept this relationship experience, it transforms us into members of something larger than ourselves — and thus we expand in an always growing definition of who we are.

CHAPTER 7

Male Sexuality: Harmonizing Sex with Other Aspects of Your Life

A richer, more fulfilling, and more peaceful masculine spirituality will depend in no small measure upon new ways of learning to be sexual.
— *James B. Nelson,
from* The Intimate Connection

In recovery, we face ourselves as sexual beings. Whether we are recovering from sex addiction, drug addiction, depression, alcoholism, divorce, physical illness, or codependency, we have to deal with our sexuality. We are not fully into recovery until we acknowledge the important place our sexuality has in our lives and how important our sexual development is as a part of our total progress in recovery.

Traditional Western ideas confuse people about sexuality and spirituality because they pit the spirit in a battle against the body. The ancient Greeks first invented the concept that the spirit was separate and on a higher plane than the body. Their ideas were absorbed by early Christians and spread through the Western world. Therefore it might seem radical to combine ideas about spiritual growth with sexuality, but recovery is a spiritual process and it sweeps all aspects of our lives into its influence, including our sexuality. After we break out of the thinking that keeps our body and spirit separate and begin to think about them linked together, we get new insights that can liberate and enrich our lives.

We used the word *spirituality* in Chapter Three to mean awareness and respect for inner experience, and a feeling of connection with a power greater than ourselves. *Sex*, as the word is used in everyday language, usually refers to the act of intercourse. *Sexuality* is a much broader term than sex. It refers to all the personal and physical dimensions of being sexual. For men, sexuality is the pleasure we take in being masculine: it's being sexually attracted to another person; it's being able to do specifically male things with our bodies; it's the way we dress, and the way we talk to women and other men. Thinking spiritually, sexuality is "the desire for intimacy and communion, both emotionally and physically . . . urging, pulling, luring, driving us out of loneliness into communion, out of stagnation into creativity."[1]

This chapter is written in language for heterosexual men, but I believe homosexual men will find in this discussion appropriate principles for their lives as well.

Pervasive Turmoil about Sexuality

Turmoil and uneasiness about sexuality seem widespread. The media attention to the topic seems to be only dominated by coverage of unhealthy sexuality, such as sexual harassment and exploitive sexual acts, or about AIDS, herpes, and other sexually transmitted diseases.

The most well-known sex researchers in America, Masters and Johnson, state,

> There is little question that personal dissatisfaction with sex is commonplace in our society today. Half of all American marriages are troubled by some form of sexual distress ranging from disinterest and boredom to outright sexual disfunction. A high proportion of unmarried adults voice similar complaints about sex: they can't find partners who are "right" for them, they feel that sex is pressured rather than relaxed and pleasing, their own erotic responsivity is inhibited or frustrated in one fashion or another.[2]

In the privacy of my therapy office, many men reveal that their sex life is tension-filled, frustrating, compulsive, addictive, or demoralizing. One man may be tense about his sexual performance. Another may be so obsessed with thoughts of sex that he inappropriately introduces a sexually flirtatious tone into his relationships with women at work and among friends. Another feels fine about his own adequacy, but he is frustrated and angry about the way his sexual partnership works.

Living in an Unfair System

Women have been speaking out to us about the inequality of tasks and roles, and many of us have been painfully awakened to ways we have held more than our share of power and privilege compared to women. We have been confronted by our wives, lovers, daughters, co-workers, and our own consciences regarding our compliance with an unfair system. We were born into this system of unfairness to women, but we are responsible for our own behavior. For spiritual growth we must live by our values, and to the extent we are part of a system that diminishes or dehumanizes anyone, we are all diminished.

When men learn how to harmonize their sexuality
with other parts of their lives, they find more serenity and
can step aside from much of the turmoil around them.

As with many of the changes we have discussed in this book, one doesn't become healthy sexually simply by thinking about it or understanding the idea. Sexual problems first need to be acknowledged. Because change builds on itself and gathers momentum over time, we shouldn't be discouraged if we don't see instant results. Facing the truth and making changes is emotionally painful and frightening. Habits tempt us to return to what we know, even if it is destructive. Solutions aren't always clear — they require us to take risks with the unknown.

Yet, I know scores of men who have learned healthier ways to be sexual, healthier ways of expressing their masculinity, their sexuality, and their spirituality. They did it by including sex in their total pattern of healing. When they did, a new level of peace entered their lives and relationships.

In seeking a wholesome, spiritual, and loving sexual lifestyle,
a man has several choices.

He can make a commitment to one special woman, or, if homosexual, to one special man. He can choose to be celibate, or he can choose to be single, exploring relationships without a primary commitment. Whatever choice he makes, he brings sexuality out of its separate, supposedly nonspiritual, often secret compartment.

"I always initiate, and you always decide...."

Rita and Charlie were in marriage counseling and complained about recurring tension and conflict over sex. Rita said sex with Charlie was pleasurable, but she thought he was "oversexed." It seemed he always wanted sex, and if she wasn't interested he felt angry or hurt. Charlie said, "It's true, I'm always ready, but you're always the one who decides if we do it. I always initiate, and you always decide. That makes me feel like you control our sex life, and I resent that. I wish you would initiate sometimes." Rita replied, "Maybe I would approach you more often if you gave me time to develop an appetite. I don't feel like I control our sex life, and I don't want to be in control of it. I think your self-esteem is in your penis and you constantly need reassurance."

Rita and Charlie show a typical pattern of sexual tension. They had discussed this so many times that they knew each other's lines by heart. They always expressed the same feelings, and neither could grow from their communication because they never found a way to move to a deeper level of honesty on the subject. Each had a position and held it. Each feeling they expressed prompted the partner's predictable reaction. That was their gridlock.

As a partnership, they were stalled. A bit of surprise or change, or a deeper level of honesty by either one might have toppled them into something less predictable and opened more possibilities. Each felt helpless and thought the other had the power to create change if only he or she was willing.

When Charlie learned that being "always ready" was his half of the problem in their relationship, he recognized his need to learn new behaviors. He began to rely less on sex to resolve his tension. He learned to talk more about what he felt.

He learned more about caressing and being sensual. He learned it was possible to become aroused, but not feel cheated if they did not have intercourse or orgasm. These changes in Charlie removed the demand that Rita felt to provide relief every time he got aroused, so she felt more relaxed. Charlie accepted his sexual feelings and his arousal as a pleasurable part of being a sexual man, not Rita's job to fix. In the process, their tension diminished, they entered a phase of mutual exploration instead of mutual demands, and their sex life became more relaxed, more playful, and more fulfilling to both.

Naturally, women have their own experience of sexuality, but the topic of women's sexuality will not be dealt with here. For men to be more liberated sexually, more fulfilled and peaceful, we must first focus and learn more about our own sexuality.

> *A man's options for sexual growth need not await*
> *a change by his partner.*

Waiting for the other person to make a change as Rita and Charlie did is precisely the pattern that keeps things unchanged. We are stuck when we catch ourselves saying, "If only she would be more assertive . . . or less assertive . . . or more sexy . . . or different in some other way. Then I could be different." Or, "After my partner does this, then I'll do that, but not before!" or, "If she's willing to do her part, I'm willing to do mine."

Many men feel so dependent on their partners for their sexuality and for their satisfaction that they always look outward to deal with it. It becomes their partner's job to provide satisfaction and release, and to accept the blame for any frustration. For a man to integrate sexuality into his program of growth, he must first claim ownership of it. He lays claim to the joys of male sexual feelings and accepts the challenge of harmonizing them with the rest of his life.

A man who hasn't claimed ownership of his sexuality cannot take responsibility for it. It seems strange that a heavy word like "responsibility," which feels like a burden, also provides liberation. In the same way, the banks of a river restrict its flow, but they also provide direction and make its flow possible. Men take responsibility by making choices about how to allow their sexual expression to flow and then remaining faithful to their choices; by appreciating the impulses and aliveness in their bodies; by accepting appropriate limitations on their expression; by learning to feel comfortable with their sexuality and interacting with it as they do with any other natural appetite. Through taking personal responsibility for their sexuality, men are liberated to love and accept themselves and others.

Moralistic and puritanical ideas about sex prevent what they try to encourage.

I think most of the condemning attitudes about sex found in repressive families and fundamentalist churches are intended to create responsible sexual behavior. But what therapists have seen for several years is that rigid attitudes and religiosity can be a hotbed for secret, irresponsible sexual behavior.

Families where sexual abuse has occurred are often bound to rigid rules of behavior that are backed up by overly strict religious practices. Religious practice can be enhancing and uplifting. But, in treating family sexual abuse and the many miseries afflicting people with sexual problems, inappropriate rigidity and religiosity is often part of the life of these families. Rigidity and harsh rules create irresponsible adults who are naive and unprepared to deal with their feelings. Healthy rules can help people live a better life, but these rules should not be used to shame and condemn them.

*Not talking about sex neglects children who need help
in learning how to deal with their bodies.*

Another characteristic of families with an unhealthy attitude toward sexuality is their failure to talk about sex. Children in these families grow up and reach adulthood with a
natural sexual urge and capacity, yet they often know more
about table manners than they do about healthy sexuality.
This is like giving a sixteen-year-old boy the keys to a car
because he is old enough to drive and sending him out on a
busy highway, hoping he learns to drive from experience
before anybody gets hurt.

When a man grows up with no affirmation or acknowledgement of his sexual side, he is left alone with his
sexual urges with no means to understand them. The only
option for him is to keep sex secret, because he has no model
for harmonizing it with his relationships. As he grows up, he
may sneak all of his learning from books or pornographic
magazines and talk furtively with other boys or girls about it.
But he remains essentially alone with his feelings.

How Do Recovering Men Grow Sexually?

A recovering man grows through open, honest discussion
about sex. While he may be very interested in the topic of sex,
a recovering man may have to break through the resistance to
honest discussion that he learned in his family. He needs to
talk about all his feelings with his sexual partner, and with
other men. In *Male Sexuality*, Bernie Zilbergeld writes,

> . . . men have been and to a large extent still are,
> extensively secretive about their sexuality. They
> may joke about sex, talk a lot about this or that
> woman's characteristics and how they'd like to get
> her in bed, and make many allusions to their sexual

prowess, but, other than these bits of bravado, most men simply don't talk about sex to anyone.[3]

A man may be very comfortable watching an erotic movie or making a play for a woman, but to actually talk about how they feel is quite a different matter. Bringing up sex in honest, direct ways may raise tension, fears, pain, or shame. These feelings don't fit with what they consider a strong male image, so many men avoid the subject, fearing they will expose a weak spot and appear less of a man.

Talking about Sex Honestly

Spiritual growth happens by making connections. In talking about sex, a man makes connections with himself and with others. He develops comfort with the topic and learns how to reflect on his experiences and feelings. In the process, he reveals himself to himself. Sometimes, as a man talks, a strong feeling rises within and he exclaims, "I didn't know I felt that way until just now!" That is how he gets to know himself. Through talk with others, he borrows and shares and builds on others' experiences rather than starting from scratch like the cave man with no prior human history.

Many men in sexual turmoil grew up with no discussion or acknowledgement of sexuality, yet they had abundant sexual stimulation around them. Perhaps the stimulation came from a mother who gave seductive bedtime kisses or walked around the house in the nude. Perhaps father left pornography where his son could read it, or he made titillating, exploitive remarks about women. Or the stimulation may have come from television or from the neighbors. These situations become a double-bind for a child, because while talk about sex is denied or forbidden, he is flooded with stimulation. And because sex is not discussed, no direction or guidance is given on how to deal with the stimulation.

The child must respond in some way to the stimulation. His natural sexual urges, and his isolation in dealing with the stimulation, make him vulnerable to developing primitive, irresponsible, or abusive sexual behavior. When he becomes an adult, a man who grew up in this situation needs healing experiences to break down his isolation. He can begin to talk about his sexuality; not bragging about what he would like to do or has done, but saying honestly what he feels sexually, what his experience feels like, what moves him, what is pleasurable, what his doubts and fears are, what he has done, and what has happened to him.

The man who talks frankly in therapy, with his lover, or with close friends about his sexual life may break down barriers that existed for his whole life. Talking directly and honestly, especially with another man, may not have happened since adolescence, if ever at all. At first, it feels risky. In this phase, if the person is in therapy, a review of his sexual history can be helpful. It raises a wide range of topics that many men have never discussed with anyone before. Sexual learning and experiences from a person's earliest memories are uncovered and sexual development is traced to the present time.

Understanding Your Sexual History

The sexual history is often a revealing therapeutic experience that opens a man up at several levels.

On the first level, he may remember specific events and retrieve information he had totally forgotten. With the recovered information he might gain new understanding of himself.

On the second level, he changes how he sees what he knows. Even if he gets no new memories on the first level, he may exchange his old judgmental self-image for a new developmental self-image. That is, he sees how he became his present self, rather than believing he's defective or bad or inadequate.

The sexual history makes a man aware of his developmental process, how his life experiences affected him, how one thing led to another, and it makes clear that he still is on a path that advances his further development.

The third level opens a man to his relationships. On this level, a man literally breaks down his isolation as he speaks. He is less alone because, often for the first time, he is talking with another man about sexual thoughts, feelings, and his experiences as a man. This exchange is essential for bringing sexuality into harmony with one's life.

Much of Our Sexuality Is Learned from Other Men

We aren't born with the knowledge or experience of male sexuality. We're born with the biology. We need to learn from other people how best to fulfill the possibilities of our sexuality. But we can't learn all about masculine sexuality from women. Boys learn about masculine feelings and choices from their fathers and other men. If a boy's father was distant or not available, and didn't show the closeness for this kind of discussion, when the boy grows up he may naturally feel most comfortable talking to a woman. She can give him warmth, love, acceptance, pleasure. An adult man who continues to grow also needs honest interaction with other men — not necessarily an expert to give advice, but just another man to talk with. If he relies entirely on a woman for his learning and sexual growth, he misses something. Talking openly and vulnerably with other trusted men provides empowerment, comradery, and identification.

I have a group of men friends who have worked very hard at being honest and direct in discussing sexual issues. I admit it has not been easy, and it's a rare thing for men to do. We have had a mixture of deeply moving discussions and uproariously funny ones. On some occasions, when one of the guys talked openly about a vulnerable sexual issue or memory he had, we all identified with him and pulled together as a group because we could see ourselves in his situation. But other times, we reverted to talking in superficial and general terms, even though the ice was broken among us for more direct talk. No matter what the struggle, this open exchange between a group of men was enormously rewarding.

The sexual history review is a systematic, clinical approach to the common human need for talk about sex. While many recovering men require a specialist to guide them in the process, everyone needs the informal, do-it-yourself form of opening up with trusted friends.

The sexual history is summarized here because it might raise topics for informal discussion in breaking your own silence. This summary is not intended to be a specific guide to follow, only a list of ideas.

The Climate for Touch, Affection, and Talk in Your Childhood

- How did touch happen in your home?
- Can you recall a specific moment of being touched or held and how it felt?
- Did people touch each other affectionately?
- Did they touch in anger with hitting?
- Did the adults show affection to each other in front of the children?
- How did touch happen around daily personal care and routines at bath time, bedtime, toilet needs, or illnesses? Who helped you with these routines? Did they feel loving, caring, relaxed, pleasant? Were they ever sexually stimulating for you? Were they ever disrespectful or belittling?
- How were all these events talked about?

Early Memories of Sex or Genitals
- What do your remember from your first awareness of your penis or someone else's genitals?
- What happened?
- Who was there?
- Did you see something or did you directly experience something?
- Was it a positive, negative, or neutral experience?
- Were you sexually aroused?
- What did it mean to you?
- Did anyone help you interpret it? What did they tell you?
- How did it affect your self-esteem?

Sexuality in Childhood and Adolescence
- How did you learn about the differences between males and females?
- What did your father tell you about sex?
- What did your mother tell you?
- Did you talk about sex with other children or explore each other's bodies?
- Were you ever discovered in sexual play? What did that mean to you and how was it handled?
- When did you learn to masturbate? How frequently did you masturbate?
- Did you find pornography? How did you use it, and how did you feel about it?

Sexual Experiences with Others
- Do you recall your first crush? How old were you?
- What effect did it have on you? Did you tell anyone?

- When did you first have a date? What adolescent sexual experiences did you have with females? What happened, and what did it mean to you at the time? How do you feel now looking back on it?
- Did you have sexual experiences with other males? What happened and what did that mean to you? How do you feel now, looking back on it?

Feelings or Experiences that Troubled You

- Describe specific details of sexual situations that troubled you: who, what, when, and where? These details are the most difficult to disclose, but they are necessary to get to your true feelings.
- Was there ever a time you felt something was wrong with you or that you were misinformed or lacking in some way sexually?
- Did you ever feel guilty or ashamed of your sexual behavior? What happened and how did you deal with it?
- Did you ever feel frightened in a sexual situation? Did you ever feel that you could not control your sexual behavior? How did you try to get control?
- Did you ever feel overwhelmed? Helpless? Hopeless? Powerful or invincible?

Growing through Self-knowledge

Men in recovery develop a deeper honesty because they have faced adversity and thereby faced themselves. Self-knowledge is strength. It helps a man cope with his life in many ways. The strength of knowing yourself is unlike a show of strength that only impresses others. A man strong with self-knowledge has the solid foundation of honesty on which to stand. He knows his strengths, his weaknesses, and his problems and needs. He knows his likes and dislikes, and he knows his values.

To keep growing and to harmonize sexuality with the rest of your life, it will help to take an inventory of your sexual pleasures, needs, and problems in your adult life. Knowing yourself includes knowing what you enjoy sexually. After you think about what pleases you, it is easier to let your partner know. Telling your sexual partner what pleases you will be a very intimate conversation that may continue for years.

You and your partner can explore and experiment in your sexual relationship. The added atmosphere of candlelight or music may enhance your erotic experiences. Body massage is an excellent means of connecting with your partner and letting go of the concerns of the day. Scented oils and lotions provide enhancement to body massage. You may find certain kinds of touch to be more pleasing than others. Describe your sexual fantasies to further help identify your pleasures. The two of you may find reading to each other a book on sexual pleasures a helpful way to raise topics, to discuss and experiment with various sexual pleasures. Two excellent comprehensive reference books on sex, sexual pleasure, and problems are *Masters and Johnson on Sex and Human Loving* by William H. Masters, Virginia E. Johnson and Robert C. Kolodny, and *The Family Book About Sexuality* by Mary S. Calderone and Eric W. Johnson.

Don't Fear Problems with Sexual Function

High percentages of men recovering from chemical dependency face difficulties with sexual function. The first step in resolving these types of problems is like the First Step in AA — admit that you have a problem. For many, the problem first appears after they begin recovery. Perhaps while drinking or doing other drugs, they divorced feelings from sexuality and they performed adequately. But once they began feeling during sex, they were frightened by what they felt. Perhaps they didn't know how to experience strong feelings and be sexual at the same time. Consequently, they developed problems with impotence, premature ejaculation, or failure to achieve orgasm.

These usually are temporary conditions. In fact, it's normal for most people to experience temporary problems with sex at some time in their lives. Most problems get better if they are dealt with directly. If the problems don't improve with time, most are treatable with professional sex therapy. If the problems are denied or avoided, they can persist for years. Many men have problems with sexual function that date back long before they began to recover. A decision to finally get professional help to deal with these problems often springs from a new sense of hope men feel about life in recovery.

Before going for sex therapy, there are things you can do that may help. The best thing for any sexual relationship is to talk to your partner about your feelings. This creates the basis for intimacy that affects your sexual responses. Next, learn this lesson and keep it in mind: sex is much more than orgasm. Sometimes it takes a problem with sexual function to teach us that lesson. We may think that because of a problem with sex, we can't be sexually active, or we're afraid to start something in bed that we're not sure we can complete successfully. Many couples, however, have a satisfying, intimate, sexual time together touching, caressing, massaging, and talking without orgasm. When orgasm is not your goal and intercourse is not a performance test, you will be more free to simply enjoy each other.

As part of your development, whether you have a problem with sexual function or not, here is an interesting experience you and your partner might explore. You can agree that you will explore each other's bodies physically and sensually, without penetration or without orgasm. You will be actively physical with each other by using massages, and by caressing and playing with each other. You can enhance the experience with music and soft lights or candlelight. You would not want to do this as a permanent agreement but perhaps once, or for the next week, month or any specified period you agree upon. This reduces tension and creates a learning situation for the two of you to expand your range of what is sensual, sexual, pleasurable communication in your relationship.

A word of caution: Don't play games with yourself in this experience. That is, don't say "We'll set up the limits and then change them if we feel like it." If you decide on certain limits, stay with them even if you want to change them in the midst of passion. Think of this as your time to learn and to expand your pleasure from a different sexual experience. If you play games with your subconscious, it catches on quickly and outmaneuvers you, spoiling the benefits of the experience. You can choose to change the limits but don't do it impulsively in the heat of passion. Make a plan and change it only when you are using your rational mind.

Masturbation

Masturbation may be a good issue on which to take inventory. Many people know now that masturbation is a normal, healthy sexual expression. It is encouraging that I don't often see men in therapy thinking they should feel guilty because they masturbate. In a man's relationship with himself, he might give masturbation a meaningful place.

Yet, many men carry a burden of shame about sex in general, and they may focus it on their masturbation activities. For instance, some men have recollections of masturbating excessively in adolescence and still feel ashamed about it.

Others continue to masturbate compulsively and secretly. They don't let their sexual partner know they do it, and they try to stop or put it off, but without success. Because it is secret and compulsive, it has a negative impact on a couple's sexual relationship. Many have tried to tell themselves they should not be so ashamed, because they know masturbation is normal, but that doesn't help because it doesn't get to the heart of their shame.

It's not masturbation itself that invokes their shame, but the compulsive and secret nature of their activities. To tell such a man that masturbation is normal and not to worry is like telling the same thing to someone who compulsively washes his hands. The answer is theoretically correct, but it's not very helpful. For a man with these issues, the place to begin might be to reveal the secret. Discuss it with your sexual partner and reach an agreement about the role you want masturbation to have in your sexual partnership.

Pornography

Pornography is an issue for men that can be closely related to masturbation. It is a controversial public topic involving many conflicting definitions, values, and rights. The First Amendment of the U.S. Constitution guarantees our right to freely read and view what we choose. At the same time, many have described pornography's degrading effect on women. We men, concerned about renewal and recovery, need to be alert to the harm it can also do to us.

By pornography, I mean the use of literature or pictures that combine eroticism with disrespect. Both erotic and disrespectful aspects of an image may reside either in the image itself, how it was created and obtained, or they may be in the attitude a man brings to the picture and what it does to him. An erotic picture may not be pornographic at all when it conveys basic human dignity, is respectful of people, and evokes healthy sexual feelings in those who look at it.

For instance, a sexually explicit drawing may be joyous, respectful, and enhancing, and it can be used in that spirit, encouraging pleasure, appreciation of sexuality, self-esteem, and connection between people. Yet the same picture can be used as pornography when a man's fantasies or behavior treat the person in the picture as an object. This encourages him to objectify the women in his life. It can be used as pornography when he treats his own body as an object, leading him into isolation rather than into healthy relationships.

Large amounts of available erotic material is inherently pornographic. Much of it was obtained by exploiting those accustomed to being victims and paying them to continue their pattern of being used sexually. Some depict human beings as sex objects, as body parts, as things to be used for pleasure, rather than as persons. When men use this material, or when they use truly innocent erotic material pornographically, they may develop a harmful image of themselves and others as objects to be used, to be turned on and turned off.

As described in Chapter Three, our mental images shape us. When we repeatedly return to our images and develop them, their power increases and shapes our lives. Pornographic images dehumanize and draw men into disrespectful ideas of himself and his lover. Some men think pornography helps them grow and experience their sexuality more fully. Others say it provides a harmless release for sexual tension. I see it, however, as more than a release. Use of pornography becomes a *rehearsal* for acting disrespectfully in relationships, leading to bad communication with one's lover and increasing isolation. It leads men off the path of development and into sexual deadends rather than into the spirituality of joyful sexual expression, connection, and relationship.

" . . . pornography seduced him into a private world . . . "

Joe described his relationship with pornography as a long-term problem he ultimately had to end if he was to renew his life. He only learned to relax sexually in his fantasies when he was alone with his erotic pictures. Year after year, he used magazine photographs for sexual release. He developed exciting relationships with women in his fantasies, but he became less and less able to have a rewarding, intimate relationship with his wife, Carol. He could be sexual, but he was so guarded that he wasn't emotionally present. His relationship with her felt tense because it naturally had the risk of surprise, disagreement, and rejection.

Joe's pornography seduced him into a private world with intensity and release, but no risk. He could control that world because his will always went unchallenged. It encouraged him to avoid the risks of real intimacy. He became highly critical of Carol, and blamed her for his unhappiness and loneliness.

When he arrived in therapy to talk about his unhapppiness, he quickly uncovered feelings of unworthiness and fears in his relationships with women. The more Joe continued to use pornography for sexual release, the more he felt he was betraying himself by not risking a real relationship with Carol. That is where his relationship with pornography became obvious. He decided to end it so he could be more available for true intimacy.

In *A Male Grief: Notes on Pornography and Addiction*, an outstanding essay, David Mura, describes how the user of pornography abuses himself and can become addicted to it.

He writes that a boy who was treated disrespectfully or abused may grow up perpetuating his own disrespect or abuse by using pornography. The stimulation of pornography can be used to cover other feelings, and he can become addicted to it. Mura writes, "At the essence of pornography is the image of flesh used as a drug, a way of numbing psychic pain."[4]

We have said that the link between sexual and spiritual growth is in relationships. The addictive power of pornography is great because the control a man feels over his pleasure can be so great. Using it, he is not challenged by dialogue with another person. He has absolute control over when he brings out the images, what he does with them, what he imagines them to be like, and when he puts them away again. Mura writes,

> The addiction to pornography is not fun. Underneath all the assertions of liberty and "healthy fun" lie the desperation and anxiety, the shame and the fear, the loneliness and sadness, that fuel the endless consumption of magazines and strip shows, x-rated films, visits to prostitutes. If addicts portray themselves as hedonists or carefree, this portrayal is belied in those moments and feelings they do not let anyone else see.[5]

Learning to Love Ourselves

We must love ourselves to have a spiritual outlook on sexuality, to take responsibility for it, and to harmonize it with our lives. As we enjoy expressing our sexual selves, sexuality draws us into the human circle of contact. Spiritual sexuality means we have humility and dignity, and we take pleasure in our sexuality as God's creative gift to our relationships.

CHAPTER 8

The Demons and Pitfalls of Recovery

Fears are educated into us,
and can, if we wish,
be educated out.

—*Karl A. Menninger*

There are pitfalls along the recovery journey that can cause us to stumble, and demons that come out from hiding places to scare us or throw us off course. In discussing them, I feel somewhat like a wilderness guide. We are out on the trail, following this alternative lifestyle called recovery, and there are some hard-won secrets to learn that have been gleaned from the struggles and painful experiences of other recovering men on our path. We want to be successful on our journey. It is not good to be naive or unprepared for the challenges we face. In this chapter, we'll talk about some things that can help us and strengthen us along the way.

While there is no way to anticipate all the pitfalls and demons of recovery, three main ones crop up repeatedly:

- anxiety,
- depression, and
- shame.

If you can anticipate these difficulties, with understanding and time, they can be neutralized or even turned to your gain; your trouble can turn out to be a blessing and a teacher.

". . . the buzz of an electrical shock coursed through my body . . . "

An experience of mine illustrates how some of these difficulties can work against recovery. My two daughters, who were twelve and fifteen years old, and I went on a vacation to Devil's Tower, Wyoming. We were part of a group aiming to climb the sheer rock wall that thrusts hundreds of feet above the Wyoming landscape. It is an awesome natural wonder that was featured in the movie, *Close Encounters of the Third Kind*. Our own encounter was to be the direct, physical kind, using ropes and very safe techniques, under the leadership of experienced mountain climbers.

On the day of our climb, we started at the first light of dawn, walking to the base of Devil's Tower. By three o'clock in the afternoon we reached the top and felt elated by the heights we achieved. But we could see a thunderstorm gaining strength on the Western horizon. It was only a small part of the landscape at the time, but because we were so high, we could see for perhaps fifty miles. Yet we knew it was potentially very dangerous for us. The height of a rock tower in a thunderstorm draws lightning and creates a very hazardous situation for climbers.

Our concerns about the thunderstorm proved valid as the dark clouds grew larger and drifted directly toward us during our hour and a half descent down the rock face. Descent by rapelling is not physically strenuous and we were accustomed to it, so whatever fear we felt, we could put in our back pockets and not waste precious minutes fretting before continuing down the rope. Still, my tension mounted. We quickly tied each knot and quickly untied them, readying the ropes for each stage of our descent, yet we took precious extra moments to double-check each procedure since our lives depended on doing it correctly. We were clearly racing against the storm that was closing in on us. The sound of thunder grew louder and began to crack.

Finally, we reached the bottom of the wall just as heavy lightning and thunder moved in. Huge rain drops pelted us and the rock around us. The main descent was completed. But we still stood on the talus, a pile of boulders at the bottom of the tower, and we had to carefully climb down them without the aid of ropes.

My daughters and I stood with our bodies braced against the rain and wind. Suddenly, there was a bright flash of lightning and the buzz of an electrical shock coursed through my body, stinging my hands and feet wherever I made contact with the rock. The jolt was just short of painful. One daughter screamed in terror, "It hit me!" Then the other one replied, "It hit me too, you're okay!" I was both panicked about what had just occurred and reassured that since they were both able to scream, they were still okay. Still, here we were standing in a place where lightning had just struck. The chances of it happening again were dreadfully high. It was crucial to get away before lightning struck again, but to move fast or carelessly was also dangerous. The stakes were as big as they could get: the lives of my two daughters and myself were on the line. I hurriedly set up a rope for the girls to use in descending a fifteen-foot ramp, and my youngest got a painful rope burn on her hands. But we got out safely.

Everyone in our climbing party received about the same amount of shock — not enough to injure them, but enough to scare them. In the aftermath, we took showers, got on dry clothes, and carried through with our plan to go out for a celebration steak dinner. Around the table, most everyone was laughing and chattering about the frightening experience.

I tried to join in, but felt somber. I felt a deep responsibility for the safety of my daughters, and I had been terrorized by the threat of harm to them. It wasn't logical, but the threat tapped into my feelings of inadequacy. I couldn't solidly guarantee my daughters' safety. The situation said to me, "You can't do your job, Merle!" It showed me the limits of my abilities. As we sat around the table I was grateful we all were safe and proud of my daughters' response to crisis. Yet, my inner sense of security and my feeling that I was a good father was deeply shaken.

That night, I crawled into my sleeping bag utterly exhausted, but the moment I closed my eyes I was right back in that impossible situation. The images played over and over again in my mind. My thoughts raced, and I tried to resolve the dilemma in my mind better than I had in the real situation. I tried to let it go and say, "Thank God, we are all safe!" But as soon as my eyes closed again, I was right back there, tense and troubled. This went on for perhaps an hour before I finally fell into a restless sleep.

Every night for weeks, I was propelled back to the impossible spot with all the bad feelings. Gradually, it got better. My self-esteem was less assaulted as I made peace with the impossibility of my task, and I let go of the terror. But to this day, every time I am exposed to the crack of thunder and lightning, I get a deep surging sense of dread. The combination of anxiety and shame that rises in me is similar to the feelings many men face in recovery. The example is clearer than many men have in recovery because its trigger was specific and identifiable. In clinical terms, I had a post-traumatic stress disorder and a remaining phobia about lightning. I was fortunate to have a supportive wife and friends who were interested and listened to me talk about what happened. My understanding of what was occurring psychologically also helped me cope with it. The residual phobia is mild enough to be no problem now.

Post-traumatic stress can appear as intense irrational feelings of anxiety, shame, and self-doubt, or a phobia that severely limits one's life. If that were true for me, I might still be worrying daily about the weather, checking forecasts for storms, getting anxious at the mere thought of a thunderstorm, restricting my activities to avoid the loss of control that the anxiety brings, and canceling contacts with friends when I thought there was even a remote possibility of a storm.

Accepting Our Lack of Control

The first step on the journey of recovery is to accept that we do not control life; the rest of our journey is to learn how to go forward, accepting our insecurity. Much is said of the rewards and the peace that recovery brings, but that picture is incomplete if we leave out the challenges and pain. Usually, the crisis that propels a man into recovery is the loss of reliable security, or loss of something that served as a reliable and secure "friend." He might have lost the false security provided by addiction, codependent behavior, or an image of security like having a good job or a loving spouse. Whatever he lost, it insulated him from insecurity. The loss may reverberate in many parts of his life, and integrating its lessons may take years. But in recovery, he becomes more aware of reality.

His transformation is a long process of learning how to maintain serenity while being aware of reality.

Life confronts us in countless ways. After we see so clearly how vulnerable we are, it often takes a long time to learn to live peacefully with our lack of control. This human problem — how to live serenely amid life's insecurity and losses — is a central issue that people have struggled with for thousands of years. The world's great spiritual traditions speak to us about it and have developed disciplines or paths to follow in response.

We often become too insulated by what we use as our security base, too protected by a single answer, to learn how to cope with insecurity. We may unconsciously scramble for an inner feeling of control, security, or comfort and thus develop compulsions to provide a structure to cope with our insecure world. Now, in the midst of making genuine progress in recovery, we still may develop anxiety, depression, or shame. But we are more honest, although we are still in the process of learning how to live with insecurity and powerlessness.

Some men get depressed for a while as they learn to accept their lack of control. The progress they've made in recovery allows them to see the insecurities of life, and the normal human response is to deeply grieve the endings and separations that are part of seeing this.

Shame also sometimes rises to the surface as a man learns to accept his lack of control. He may revert to his old stress responses and feel, *I must be a bad person for being so out of control and so vulnerable*. A man in this position must remind himself that he simply needs more time to learn how to have serenity with his truth.

As I stated at the beginning of this chapter, there are three psychological problems that men commonly encounter in recovery: anxiety, depression, and shame. I'd like to go into specifics about each one.

ANXIETY

A common factor in problems with anxiety is a struggle with control and vulnerability. We will look at panic attacks, phobias, obsessions, and compulsions. A *panic attack* is a sudden overwhelming feeling that one is out of control of himself or his circumstances. It is accompanied by physical symptoms where the person may

- feel light-headed or dizzy,
- perspire, or get suddenly hot or chilled,
- get a tingly feeling in his hands and feet,
- feel confused and unable to think,
- fear that he will faint, or go crazy, or do something he can't control,
- get a dry mouth and throat,
- develop a pounding heart and fear he is having a heart attack,
- develop rapid and shallow breathing, which often leads to hyperventilation,
- develop a nervous or upset stomach, and
- develop chest pain or discomfort.

A *phobia* is an irrational fear of an object or situation. My fear of lightning is a mild, specific phobia. Other common examples are fear of closed spaces (claustrophobia), fear of heights (acrophobia), and fear of water (aquaphobia). A person's reaction to the feared object or situation may vary from mild anxiety to panic. The man suffering from a phobia knows his fears are extreme but knowing this does not help. The fearful thoughts come when stimulated by the situation or object, and he may think his only way to gain control is to avoid the problem.

A *social phobia* is an excessive, irrational fear that a particular action will be noticed by others in public. The person who suffers from this type of phobia is extremely anxious about the reaction of others to normal behavior like eating in public, urinating in a public rest room, signing one's name while being watched. They fear they will be humiliated or embarrassed, and they avoid these situations.

Agoraphobia "is a marked fear or avoidance either of being alone or of being in certain public places. It is . . . strong enough to significantly limit the individual's normal activities. . . . The fearful thoughts that plague the agoraphobic often center around loss of control. The person may fear the development of uncomfortable physical symptoms familiar from past experiences (such as dizziness or rapid heartbeat). He may then worry that these symptoms could become worse than they were in the past . . . and/or that he will become trapped or confined in some physical location or social situation (such as a restaurant or party). In the first two situations, the person senses that his body is out of control. In the third, he feels unable to readily control his surroundings."[1]

As agoraphobia gets more severe, a person's attempt to gain control may lead him to refuse to travel more than a few miles from home, or even to refuse to leave his house. He may so restrict his life that he loses contact with friends and stops participating in supportive activities. He trades self-esteem and opportunities for growth and enrichment for the feeling of greater control over his life. Some therapists have noted a connection between a childhood in an alcoholic family and problems with agoraphobia.

Obsessions are repetitive thoughts that produce no new understanding and lead to no resolution. Their primary unconscious purpose may be to create a feeling of control while under stress. The images of myself in the lightning situation that kept coming back to my mind for weeks after the event were obsessions. Other, more common obsessions have to do with self-doubt: *Did I lock the door when I left?* Or, *Did I unplug the coffee maker?* They may feel like haunting demons because when we try to resolve them, they seem to pop up again, almost automatically. While the individual knows his thoughts are irrational, the more he tries to force them to stop by consciously controlling them, the more powerful they become. Obsessions of violence, sexual activities, or immoral acts are most common.

A man may focus on his behavior or his obsessions and then berate himself with negative questions and statements such as, *Why did you respond so insensitively to that woman? Now you did it again! You're stupid.* Or, *You ruined your job promotion!* Or, *You're a weak man!* Or even, *You're not a man at all because of the way you think!* Beneath this suffering is an unconscious belief that constant worrying gives a measure of control, that thinking about it will prevent it from happening.

A *compulsion* is a nonproductive behavior that is repeated ritually. Examples of compulsions include hand-washing several times an hour, touching certain objects, or touching them in certain ways. A compulsion, like an obsession, is a mental attempt to gain a feeling of control. The folk wisdom that says, "knock on wood to prevent bad luck when you talk about something good," takes on compulsive characteristics if a person feels anxiety or panic when he doesn't perform the ritual. Compulsion is like addiction in that tension and anxiety rise, even to the point of panic, if a person tries to stop his behavior, and both addicts and compulsive people can have well-developed rituals. R. Reid Wilson, in his book, *Don't Panic: Taking Control of Anxiety Attacks*, writes, "Unlike an alcoholic, who feels compelled to drink, but also enjoys the drinking experience, the obsessive-compulsive person achieves relief through the ritual, but no pleasure."[2]

Anxiety Is Clever and Cunning

Anxiety in its various forms is particularly difficult to overcome because of the tricks it plays on men who are wrestling with issues of control. Once the door is opened to one of these symptoms, the more directly you try to close it, the more you get caught up in the mental power struggle with it. You use your energies in puzzling and unproductive ways, trying to control what cannot be controlled.

The puzzle of anxiety reminds me of a horse our family once owned. Chief was a peaceful, friendly horse who loved attention, but if he thought you wanted to ride him, he ran all over the pasture to avoid you. I recall chasing him until I became exhausted and gave up. But if I pretended that I just happened to be walking through the pasture with some grain, but had no particular interest in him, and if I kept my rope and bridle hidden under my shirt, he would walk right up to me.

The moral of Chief's lesson to me is: Don't focus directly on control, use some finesse and you might get the peace of mind you're seeking. Rather than focusing your thoughts on what's wrong with you and trying to figure that out, give some time to what's good about you. You have the same right as everyone else to make mistakes and learn from them.

You may need to consciously restrain yourself from leaping to quick fixes for anxiety. Tell yourself it's all right to flow with your stream of feelings instead of controlling them. It's like learning how to float on your back in water. A bit of trust and a bit of tolerating the discomfort allows you to learn the technique. Take on the role of a reassuring father to your unconscious self, and say to yourself, *You can survive strong feelings. Fear is a feeling and feelings won't hurt anybody. I believe in you!*

It's Okay to Be a Beginner

Many men in recovery are just learning to release feelings that in the past were always controlled, suppressed, or covered by compulsive behavior or addictions. They've made the progress that allows these feelings to surface, but they are only beginners in dealing with them. What feels to one man like normal sadness, may feel like a flood of overpowering grief to a man who has little prior experience with feelings of loss. What feels like pleasurable openness and connection in sexual contact for one man, may feel like sudden, overwhelming exposure, with the threat of falling apart to the man who has just learned to accept his feelings. But as a man becomes more familiar with his feelings, he won't be as threatened or surprised by them. He will notice that he can say to himself, *I can feel my anger rising now. I need to respond to the signal I'm getting.* Or, *I am feeling warm and affectionate; I'll enjoy it and express it to my lover when I get a chance.*

Peace Can Present New Problems

As much as peace is desired, one needs to learn how to accept it. If I have spent years pushing against a wall and suddenly the wall is gone, I may fall on my face. I may have hated that wall, but I may feel I'm not in control when it's gone, because the wall focused my energies. With it there to push against, I knew what to do and how to do it. After it is gone, I may feel disoriented for a while.

The recovering man may feel he is out of control or at loose ends when the tension, crises, and problems he struggled with for years are gone. Calm and peace were what he wanted, but after they settle in, he is without a focus for his energy, his activity, and his will. He may develop anxiety, compulsions, or self-abusive obsessions in his attempts to regain a feeling of safety and control. Now he needs to learn on a deeper level how to go with the flow, how to trust that he can survive without forcing his will upon life. This new problem, as difficult or stressful as it may be, is a positive sign of progress on his recovery journey. He must submit to an image of himself as a good man and learn that he can be safe even if he is not in control.

Words of Caution

A few words of caution are needed because some addictive men develop secondary addictions. The alcoholic, for example, might have struggled hard with alcohol, and living without it feels much better. Now is the time another addiction may seduce him into the familiar comforting feeling of control. Many recovering addicts become addicted with equal intensity to something else that has an equal ability to consume their lives and to damage their relationships. It's common to see recovering addicts turn to a new addiction: work, food and sugar, sex, or something else to regain a feeling of control. In a book called *The Addictive Personality: Roots, Rituals, and Recovery*, Craig Nakken describes the addictive process as essentially an attempt to control the uncontrollable cycles in life.[3] He shows how a person can develop an addictive personality and, even after he gives up one addictive behavior, he falls into another one if he doesn't face his underlying desire to gain control.

Some Suggestions for Dealing with the Problems of Anxiety

Have some patience, but not too much. If you've just begun to experience an anxiety problem early in your recovery, it may be a temporary result of the many changes you are going through. By all means, tell others what it is like for you, and you probably will get relief just by talking. One discussion about your feelings is definitely not enough — you will have to do it many times. You may need reassurance from your friends that you will be okay, or that your direction in life is okay. Don't be afraid to ask them for it. It is also very reassuring to talk to another man who has faced these issues before, and has resolved them, whether they were exactly like the problems you're dealing with or are slightly different.

Focus Your Mind on Your Breathing

In the midst of a panic attack, your symptoms may get much more frightening if you hyperventilate. This means your breathing becomes so shallow and rapid that you don't exchange the air in your lungs to get fresh oxygen. Many men have rushed to the hospital because they feared they were having a heart attack, when they were actually hyperventilating. Breathing into a paper bag, taking long, slow breaths, concentrating on exhaling fully and slowly to make room for fresh oxygen — all these can be remarkably calming. I find that concentration on my breathing, and taking slow, deep breaths is a calming exercise under any kind of stress.

Flinging Tensions and Worries to the Wind

A friend of mine gets relief from a ritual he developed to let go of his tension and worries. First, he writes the name of his worry or fear on a piece of paper. Then, he flushes it down the toilet, or he tears the paper into small shreds and goes to an upstairs window and throws them out, watching them slowly flutter away in the wind. After that, he sits back, closes his eyes, and imagines himself in a safe and peaceful place without tension. Sometimes he creates a mental image of a sack in which he places his worry and then, in his mind, he drags the burdensome sack to the very top of a high mountain and flings it into the wind.

If you have a task or activity that gives you stress, try to create a visual image of yourself in that situation successfully doing the task, and perhaps enjoying it. Public speaking creates anxiety for me, and I use this technique to calm my jitters. For a few minutes a day, several days before a speech, and sometimes just an hour before, I settle myself into a comfortable chair. Then, I relax, close my eyes, and imagine myself before my audience. I create the details of the scene in my mind: the color of walls in the room, where I am standing in relation to the audience, and an image of myself enjoying the audience and feeling articulate. It is a very effective method and can be transferred to many other stressful situations, such as a job interview, taking a test, going on a date, or driving a car. If you limit your activities and restrict your life to relieve anxiety, you have adopted too much patience with it. You have built the problem into your lifestyle, and adjusted yourself to it, not resolved it. Get professional psychotherapy if your anxieties and obsessions persist. The longer you live with them, the more entrenched they become and the more your growth and development gets stalled or sidetracked.

DEPRESSION

Many men in recovery suffer from depression, and I think that for many men, it's a necessary passage into a better life. It's like the grief that must follow the death of a loved one before you can continue your life. In its mildest form, depression may be a general sense of sadness, discouragement, and disillusionment. In its most extreme form, depression is despair beyond hope.

A correlation between alcoholism and depression has been established for years. Some experts believe that persons suffering from depression are more subject to alcohol dependency because of their tendency to medicate themselves with alcohol. Their depression gets complicated by a growing addiction to the chemical. Even when the drinking stops, the underlying depression often returns. Perhaps a bio-chemical readjustment occurs after sobriety that induces depression. Men recovering from other life transitions also seem to have a tendency to develop depression.

After having made a major turn in life, men naturally look back with a more open vision and see new things. Sometimes they feel grief about what they didn't get as children, or abuses they suffered in the past return as a dark burden. They may feel grief or the loss of a marriage and family. The passage of time and wasted years may weigh heavily. Guilt about behavior and choices that had hurtful consequences for others can come crashing in with more power than ever before. These feelings don't usually come one at a time, but in combination, and each grief reminds a person of other griefs. They can snowball, giving a man the sensation of being out of control.

A man may be depressed and not know it if he isn't in tune with his feelings. Common symptoms of depression are

- weight loss or weight gain,
- insomnia,
- difficulty getting going in the morning,
- constant fatigue,
- headaches or chest pains without organic cause,
- constipation,
- difficulty concentrating, and
- feelings of sadness or hopelessness.

Depression in recovery may be temporary and no cause for alarm. Time is a natural healer. But a man's way of dealing with it is important. Depression tugs a person toward isolation from others. If he follows that tug, he can get more and more cut off from the affectionate, supportive, and healing relationships in his life. It is a challenging period to live through, and it is crucial that he stay in close communication with people around him. When he handles it as a common human problem, and maintains his connection with others, he can grow from it.

Ways of Dealing with Depression

Sometimes depression does not seem to be related to specific events in a person's life. A man might say, "I've got everything going for me in my life, but I feel miserable." The interplay of psychology, life experience, and biology is a complex field where new discoveries are being made, and there is much to learn about depression from these discoveries. We know biological factors influence how one feels — and life experiences can change one's biological balance. Some research suggests that there may be a strong organic aspect to depression and when there is, medication can help bring body chemistry into balance and lift the mood. Medication may serve as a bridge to the time when a person returns to a more natural organic balance.

Alcohol is a depressant and anyone troubled with depression should avoid it. Also, aerobic exercise has shown to be an effective treatment for depression. Any physical exertion that moderately raises your breathing and heart rate for twenty minutes at a time, at least three or four times a week, will have a positive effect on your mood and your tension level. Walking, swimming, jogging, raquetball, and bicycling are a few good options. Check with your doctor to be sure that you are in good enough physical condition to start such a program.

SHAME

For some men, shame looms larger in recovery than it ever did before. I raise the issue of shame here again because it is a

notable pitfall in recovery, and it is closely related to the
anxiety and depression issues. As we described it in Chapter
Four, shame is a feeling that something is wrong with our
worth as a person. Becoming more aware of our feelings is
progress, and it makes us feel more vulnerable sometimes.
Our old responses may tell us that if we feel vulnerable, something must be wrong with us, so our shame is triggered.

Shame begets more shame. A man can become obsessed
with it, repeatedly undermining his manhood, value, and
competence. As painful as this is, shame becomes the new
focus for his energies, the new wall to push against. He may
feel shameful about his job and career, parenting, or marriage.
In doing so, he might feel chronically unhappy and depressed.

*"He was afraid he might behave inappropriately with the women at
work ... "*

One man came to therapy because he repeatedly
got mental images that made him feel shameful. He
pictured himself being nurtured and cared for by the
women he supervised. In therapy, it became clear
that he felt tension about managing his time and his
feelings. He had learned to care about these women
and was afraid he might behave inappropriately
with them. His shame served as a primitive control
over his impulses. He knew how to live with shame
from years of experience with it, but he didn't know
if he could deal with his new feelings of friendship
and attraction toward women at his job.

A man in recovery is always learning to deal with his feelings. Under stress, we are all tempted to return to what is old
and familiar, even if it is painful and destructive. It may be
unfamiliar for a man to stay loving and affirming toward
himself under stress. Impulsively, he reverts to old reactions

and becomes mentally self-abusive. When this happens, his problem is not the issue he focuses on, like shame about his job, or feelings of inadequacy as a father, or feeling his appearance is ugly. The problem is that under stress he almost automatically turns to negative feelings that are intense. It seems to give a similar feeling of control as some of the phobias and compulsions described earlier. The shame feelings are certainly painful, but they create a familiar feeling in the midst of stress.

Turning the Demons of Recovery into Affirmations and Strength

When you can see the pitfalls of recovery for what they are — signs of progress and challenges that can deepen your growth — you can stand back from yourself to take a detached spiritual perspective. Then, you can say, *I am challenged now to find a healthy response to this moment. I need to react in ways I could not even imagine in the past.*

I described recovery earlier as a journey that begins when we accept the fact that we do not control life. This journey continues as we learn, in spite of our insecurity, how to go forward as an active participant in life. Fear of the demons and pitfalls of anxiety, depression, and shame are the ways many of us learn our lessons, and deepen our recovery. They challenge us to accept again, and more deeply, life's insecurities and to fully participate in life in spite of the risks.

Epilogue: Following a Pattern of Daily Growth

> Try not to become a man of success,
> Rather become a man of value.
> — *Albert Einstein*

I think there are two kinds of growth experiences: the *eye-opening experience* of becoming newly aware, and the longer, slower work of *learning how to live well*. Eye opening is the revealing of truth and admitting it. Learning how to live well is the application of truth in our lives and building skills.

Balancing Two Kinds of Growth

I know from my therapy practice and from my private life that both types are crucial for continued growth. If we rely entirely on one kind of growth, we get lopsided, like the tree that grows branches only on one side and becomes bent. For instance, if we rely entirely on eye-opening experiences, we may think that we only need to find the right answer, the deeper truth, the best attitude, the brilliant insight, and then life will be better. Looking for answers can be like looking for a fix. It becomes a roller coaster existence until we learn the down-to-earth daily skills for living a good life. If we rely entirely on learning how to live well, we may get bogged down in rules and routines for living and fail to perceive the deeper realities or truths in our lives.

Eye-Openers

Eye-opening experiences break through our confusion and denial. They may come suddenly in blazing moments of insight, or gradually, almost imperceptibly, as dawn overtakes the night. Sometimes we call these events insights, enlightenment, conversion, hitting bottom, or gaining better perspective. They can come as painful moments when all our attempts to evade truth and reality are used up, and we finally have to surrender. They can come as rich, full moments of awe, when we realize the grace, love, and beauty that surround us.

As children, many of us thought our fathers or our heroes had control over their lives — and we too would have control when we reached their age. From a childlike perspective, we thought we would gain control over our lives when we became "emancipated, wage-earning men." I believe we leave childhood and join the world of truly adult men through the doorway of pain and difficulty — when our eyes are opened to the facts that life is difficult and that no man ever achieves so much control that he can permanently sidestep pain or avoid all awkwardness, loss, and chaos. Many of us have come to that threshold and felt pain or crisis repeatedly, but we backed away, holding tightly to our childhood perspective, refusing to change. Until we take our individual life story, our own pain and difficulty and pay attention to them — until we become honest with ourselves and accept our powerlessness — we don't pass through the doorway into adult manhood.

After gaining a grown man's humility, we know we still have a path of development stretching out before us that never ends. We know that we are vulnerable to turning from our main path to merrily follow what appear to be exciting trails but turn out to be dead ends. We are subject to pitfalls and demons all along this path. All points of arrival, all moments of completion, all fixes, all cures are just temporary resting places. They need constant revision and additional learning and polishing as we gain more life experience, as we travel further along the path.

Eye-opening experiences point us in new directions, motivate us, and change our attitudes. They lead us to say, "I'm not going to live this way any longer!" Or, "I have a lot to be grateful for!" But, once they point us toward a better life, they can't teach us *how* to do it. Realizing we need to recover, we next need to learn the skills for living a better life. We need to know how to be a friend; how to find serenity while knowing we can't control life; how to avoid the attractive but destructive detours and dead ends on our paths; how to become men of value.

Learning How to Live Well

Living well provides the "how-to's." It is the art and craft of recovery. We learn to live well the same way we gain skill for any art or craft — from others who serve as our coaches or teachers, and by the daily routine of practice, discipline, and hard work. After listening to someone play the piano, you may passionately want to learn it for yourself. But it won't happen from a sudden rush of desire, or even from talent alone. Desire is necessary, and a belief that you can do it is necessary, but you also need lessons and hours and hours of practice to play well.

I assume that any man who has the interest to read this book is in recovery. By my reckoning, any truly adult man is, in some way, a recovering man. Developing skills for living well is an important part of our progress at this place in our recovery. Skill is knowing how to change and maintain that part of our lives we *can* control.

Throughout this book, I've discussed the ingredients of recovery for men. The main message of this Epilogue is to make it clear that no one works with the ingredients just once and that no one possesses all of them. Instead, we incorporate them into a daily lifestyle of recovery. As we do, we maintain our adventure of continued growth, gradually becoming more well-defined individuals, knowing ourselves better, tasting life more fully, deepening our values. We find serenity and let go of what is beyond our control, and humbly take our place as participants in creation.

A slip or a relapse for a man with an addiction is serious business. It can be fatal. I have heard more than once, "I don't know if I have one more recovery in me if I slip again." We know that sobriety begins by refraining from the addictive agent or behavior. Replacing it with a lifestyle of growth assures continued progress. At the least, a relapse is a loss of time and progress in our development. If a slip or a relapse occurs, it is not a time to sink into shame and guilt, but a time for eye opening, to take notice, to learn from our experience so we can prevent another one.

Following are some guidelines for recovery. They are the guidelines I use in my life and that I recommend to my clients. I have not found a way to state them that satisfies me completely or that seems comprehensive, but I offer them as one man's imperfect attempt to assemble guidelines for progress in recovery. They come from many sources: some from recent medical research; some from the wisdom of Twelve Step programs; some from psychology; and some from ancient spiritual traditions.

Just as you might work out daily to develop physical conditioning, you can practice these guidelines for recovery to establish your skills for living well. Men who are already in Twelve Step recovery programs will find that these guidelines support their program but cannot replace it. Men who don't have a recovery group would find a buddy system helpful — an agreement with one or more male friends to support your recovery. You could do that by meeting weekly at a regular time and place to talk about your experiences with the guidelines, and your recovery in general. You may have important additions or changes that fit your individual situation. I encourage you to use your own wisdom to add to, modify, or rearrange the guidelines.

GUIDELINES FOR DAILY MAINTENANCE AND PROGRESS IN RECOVERY

Emotional Self-care

- Talk to someone on a personal level every day. Develop close relationships. Maintain them with frequent contact, and mend them when there is a problem. Have at least one or two friends who know your life story, who you bring into your home at times, and with whom you can be unguarded.
- Stop every day to tune in to your feelings. Let yourself feel them, talk to someone about them, and listen to how others feel. All feelings are acceptable. Make choices about how you express them.
- Be honest with yourself and others. Honesty is the foundation of mental health and recovery.
- Avoid self-pity. Life is difficult, and self-pity distracts you from the real work of life and recovery.

- Use rituals to mark life transitions. Rituals are ways to let go and to notice change. They build self-esteem and transform the past into a hopeful, stronger future. Grieve your losses. Celebrate anniversaries, holidays, birthdays, achievements, and life changes. You might light a candle, plant a tree, take a day off, sing a song, invite a friend for dinner, attend religious services, send a letter, put up a sign, give a gift, have a party, make an object, write a poem, or take a walk.
- Be alert for shame. When you notice it, look for the pain beneath it so it will not linger to erode your self-esteem.
- Keep a journal for writing down important events in your life. Reflect on them, and get to know yourself and observe your growth over time.

Physical Self-care

- Do aerobic activity at least three or four times a week for a minimum of twenty minutes. Exercise vigorously enough to increase your breathing and heart rate and cause you to sweat (provided it is physically safe for you to do so). Try walking, running, biking, or swimming. Check with a doctor before you begin.
- A daily stretching routine will help you relax and stay fit and flexible. You may combine it with moderate sit-ups, push-ups and weightlifting.
- Eat well. A healthy diet contains foods that are low in fat, salt, and sugar and high in fiber and complex carbohydrates. Make your meal a time to savor the tastes; eat slowly and enjoy the company of your family or friends. Don't eat while doing something else, such as reading, driving, or watching television.

Spiritual Self-care

- Take the risk to believe you can recover. Remind yourself once a day that your life can be better, that you can have self-esteem. If you don't believe it, then act as if you do so you can proceed with the work of recovery.
- Find your refuge. Identify a place or an activity that you know will help you relax and feel safe. Return to it regularly. It might be special music, a sport, nature, talking to friends, movies, books, et cetera.
- Take twenty minutes each day to meditate, pray, or do creative visualization. It relaxes you, helps you develop a connection with your Higher Power, and trains you in concentration and letting go.
- Give your creativity an outlet. Find ways to create or build things that give you pleasure. Work with wood, help others, play music, write in a journal, coach a children's sport, plant a garden, take up photography, et cetera.
- Take one day at a time. When you find yourself wanting to go faster, feeling impatient for progress, or worrying about the future or the past, stop and return your attention to the present moment — the only moment you can actually be in.
- Make room for humor, laughter, jokes, and play. Learn to gain access to the healing and refreshing power of the light side.
- Select someone you are willing to account to for your recovery program. You might choose a friend, a sponsor, a counselor, a spiritual advisor, or a therapist, and talk to him or her regularly about your progress.

When I learned to meditate by concentrating on my breathing, my instructor advised me that distracting thoughts would continually enter my mind. To develop skill I should learn not to fight with the distractions, but simply let them go and return my concentration to my breathing. That is how I think about these guidelines. Don't expect a single day in which you follow them perfectly. But keep coming back to them anyway. They won't help you achieve perfection, but they will help you build on what you have done so far and remain on the recovery path.

Following these guidelines opens us up to more eye-opening experiences and to our powers of wisdom and intuition. They keep us alert to life. Some of us can only select one or two of the guidelines to follow because of other responsibilities to family, job, and community, and this may be sufficient. As we live with them, we may gradually incorporate more of them as routines in our lives.

We don't always notice the benefit of these activities while we are doing them. But our skill in following them, and their benefit in our lives intensify over months of faithful practice. One day, we notice we aren't as tense, or our relationships are deeper and more peaceful, or we're much more effective on our job.

Linking Emotions, Body, and Spirit

The distinctions between emotional, physical, and spiritual self-care are purely artificial, and I use them only to make it easier to talk about. They all blend together in a man's progress. For instance, the aerobic exercise listed under physical self-care has excellent emotional benefits, and the meditation listed under spiritual self-care is helpful physically in reducing blood pressure, and increasing coronary health, as well as helping other healing.

Albert Einstein's wisdom at the opening of the Epilogue is an excellent guide for men's recovery and for development of self-esteem. Certainly, Einstein was a success by any measure, but in his wise, spiritual perspective, he says that was not his primary goal. He counsels us, "Try not to become a man of success, rather become a man of value." Another way to say it might be: don't work so hard to do something or control matters outside yourself, rather work to become the kind of man you want to be. When I think about masculine recovery as an art or a craft, I consider my daily life to be a continual process of developing, creating, and shaping the design for being a "man of value."

Endnotes

Chapter One

1. Barbara Sullivan, "Getting in Touch," *Chicago Tribune*, Wednesday, 26 October 1988, 7.
2. Dennis Wholey, *The Courage to Change* (Boston: Houghton Mifflin Company, 1984), 41.
3. Russell Baker, Foreword in *About Men: Reflections on the Male Experience*, Edward Klein and Don Erickson, eds. (New York: Poseidon Press, 1987), 9.

Chapter Two

1. Shunryu Suzuki, *Zen Mind, Beginner's Mind* (New York: Weatherhill, 1970), 21.
2. Jesse Glen Gray, *The Warriors* (Harcourt, 1959), 26.
3. Ibid., 36.
4. Ibid., 27.
5. Baker, Foreword in *About Men*, 10.
6. Scott Campbell with Phyllis Silverman, *Widower* (New York: Prentice Hall Press, 1987), 216.
7. Leslie H. Farber, *Lying Despair, Jealousy, Envy, Sex, Suicide, Drugs, and the Good Life* (New York: Basic Books, 1976).
8. Frederick Franck, "Notes on the Koan," *Parabola* vol. 13, no. 3 (August 1988): 33, 36.
9. Ibid., 35.
10. Stephen Foster with Meredith Little, *The Book of the Vision Quest* (New York: Prentice Hall Press, 1980).
11. Sue Serrone, "Festivals," *Utne Reader* (November-December 1987): 73.

Chapter Three

1. Marion Woodman, "Worshiping Illusions," *Parabola* vol. 12, no. 2 (May, 1987): 64.
2. David Huddle, "Let's Say You Wrote Badly This Morning," *New York Times Book Review* (31 January 1988): 37.
3. Matthew Fox, public lecture in Minneapolis, Minnesota, 1985.
4. Henri J. M. Nouwen, *Reaching Out* (Garden City, N.Y.: Doubleday & Company, 1966), 97.
5. Daniel Goleman, *The Meditative Mind* (Los Angeles: Jeremy P. Tarcher, Inc., 1988).
6. Bernie S. Seigel, M. D. *Love, Medicine, & Miracles* (New York: Harper & Row, 1986).
7. Natalie Goldberg, *Writing Down the Bones* (Boston: Shambala, 1986).

Chapter Four

1. Merle A. Fossum and Marilyn J. Mason, *Facing Shame: Families in Recovery* (New York: W. W. Norton & Company, 1986).
2. F. R. Ford and J. Herrick "Family Rules/Family Life Styles," *American Journal of Orthopsychiatry.* vol. 44 (1974): 61-69.
3. Ibid.
4. Gershen Kaufman, *Shame: The Power of Caring* (Cambridge, Mass.: Shenkman Press, 1980).

Chapter Six

1. Stuart Miller, *Men & Friendship* (San Leandro, Calif.: Gateway Books, 1983), 16.
2. Jan Halper, *Quiet Desperation: The Truth about Successful Men* (New York: Warner Books, 1988), 49.

3.	James B. Nelson, *The Intimate Connection: Male Sexuality, Masculine Spirituality* (Philadelphia, Westminster Press, 1988), 49.
4.	"Loneliness found to increase likelihood of sickness, death," *Minneapolis Star Tribune* (4 August, 1988).
5.	Stuart Miller, *Men & Friendship* (San Leandro, Calif.: Gateway Books, 1983), 2-3.
6.	Ibid., 8.
7.	Erich Fromm, *The Art of Loving* (New York: Bantam Books, 1956), 84.

Chapter Seven
1.	Nelson, *The Intimate Connection,* 26.
2.	William H. Masters, Virginia E. Johnson, and Robert C. Kolodny, *Masters and Johnson on Sex and Human Loving* (Boston: Little, Brown and Company, 1986), 440.
3.	Bernie Zilbergeld, *Male Sexuality* (New York: Bantam Books, 1978), 4.
4.	David Mura, *A Male Grief: Notes on Pornography and Addiction* (Minneapolis: Milkweed Editions, 1987), 3.
5.	Ibid., 5.

Chapter Eight
1.	R. Reid Wilson, *Don't Panic: Taking Control of Anxiety Attacks* (New York: Harper & Row, 1986), 29.
2.	Ibid., 37.
3.	Craig Nakken, *The Addictive Personality* (Center City: Minn.: Hazelden Educational Materials, 1988), 3.

INDEX

wise surrender, 37-42
Suzuki, Shunryu, 23

T
Teaching of Don Juan, The
(Casteneda), 38
Therapy, 9-11, 81
Thoreau, Henry David, 112
Traumatic origin of shame,
71-72
Twain, Mark, 15
Twelve Step program, 54-55

U
Umberson, Debra, 114

V
Vision quest, 40-41
Visualization, 56-57

W
Waking up, 7-8
Weakness, 66
Wholeness, 60
Willpower, 35-37
Wilson, R. Reid, 163
Wise surrender, 37-39
exercises for, 41-42
Women, 66
Women's movement, 3
Woodman, Marion, 44
Wounded father image, 69

Writing Down the Bones
(Goldberg), 59

Z
Zen Buddhism, 38
Zilbergeld, Bernie, 140

Other titles that will interest you . . .

Touchstones
Daily Meditations for Men

The seeds of serenity and enlightenment recovering men have been waiting for. *Touchstones* encourages exploration into intimacy, masculinity, sexuality, anger, honesty, hope, prayer, self-acceptance, and commitment for men involved in any Twelve Step recovery program.
Order No. 5029   Book, 400 pp.
Order No. 5773   Audio Cassette, 60 Minutes
Order No. 5916   Book & Tape Set

Holding Back
Why We Hide the Truth about Ourselves
by Marie Lindquist

We all have things we don't like about ourselves, things we want to hide from everyone. But withholding the truth about ourselves cheats us out of love and intimacy. *Holding Back* provides a dynamic plan for accepting ourselves, and will inspire us to share ourselves with others. 168 pp.
Order No. 5012

Strong Choices, Weak Choices
The Challenge of Change in Recovery
by Gayle Rosellini and Mark Worden

Sometimes life seems to deliberately test us. And the issues we face in recovery don't always make it easy to cope. Here, the best-selling authors of *Of Course You're Angry* offer constructive advice on learning to make healthy choices. Their probing questions and checklists help us begin to understand the real-life connections between self-awareness, serenity, choice, and change. 145 pp.
Order No. 5037
